METHODOLOGY AND

Methodology and Economics

A Critical Introduction

John Pheby

Professor of Economics
City of Birmingham Polytechnic

M. E. Sharpe, Inc.
Armonk, New York

First published in the United States in 1991 by M. E. Sharpe, Inc.
80 Business Park Drive, Armonk, New York 10504

Published in Great Britain by
Macmillan Academic and Professional Ltd.

Printed in Hong Kong

Library of Congress Cataloging-in-Publication Data
Pheby, John, 1942–
Methodology and economics: a critical introduction /
John Pheby.
    p.   cm.
Includes bibliographical references and indexes.
ISBN 0–87332–851–5 (C).—ISBN 0–87332–852–3 (P)
1. Economics—Methodology.   I. Title.
HB131.P54   1991
330'.01—dc20   90–28626
                                                          CIP

To the memory of my father

Contents

Acknowledgements

Many people have helped me in the writing of this book. A particular word of thanks is due to Peter Earl and Geoff Hunt who provided me with very detailed comments and criticisms of earlier drafts. I also benefited greatly from the comments made by Bruce Caldwell, Sheila Dow and Sean O'Sullivan. Stephan Böhm provided me with much invaluable guidance in the writing of Chapter 7. To all of these people I am very grateful for their help and encouragement: needless to say I absolve them from any remaining errors and omissions.

I have also been greatly aided by my colleagues in the Department of Government and Economics for allowing me a sabbatical term to complete this project.

Finally a particular debt is owed to Barbara Abbott, who has struggled to decipher my hieroglyphics for some time. This has not prevented her from typing successive manuscripts efficiently and promptly.

JOHN PHEBY

Foreword

In recent years the attention given to methodological issues within economics has grown considerably. Several books on the subject have been published, courses established and two new journals, *Economics and Philosophy* and *Research in the History of Economic Thought and Methodology*, launched.

Why such interest? The most popular explanation argues that economics is experiencing a period of crisis. It is felt that during such periods economists tend to reflect more about what they are doing. The publication of books entitled *Why Economists Disagree, The Crisis in Economic Theory, Economics in Disarray* and *Why Economics is not Yet a Science*, suggests that something of a crisis exists. Crisis or not, there can be little doubt that the confidence acquired by economists during the post-war period has been severely shaken. Many Western industrialised nations experienced unprecedented growth and prosperity in the years following the Second World War and Keynesian demand management policies were often regarded as being primarily responsible for this economic success. This helped to foster the impression that economists had a certain degree of control over the running of the economy. Indeed budgetary policies seemingly took on the guise of 'engineering' a modest fall in unemployment or inflation. The stock of economists was probably never higher – they seemed to enjoy a public esteem unrivalled by other social sciences and it appeared that the 'dismal' science could, at last, deliver something positive and beneficial to mankind at large.

Regrettably, those halcyon days are now behind us. The growing economic malaise of the late 1960s gave way to crises that have gripped many countries through much of the 1970s and 1980s. As a result the Keynesian consensus that existed to a considerable extent during the 1950s and 1960s was shattered and this has contributed to the current situation where several alternative macroeconomic theories compete for our critical attention.

Against this background it is not surprising that many economists have turned to methodology for succour. Some feel, as Milton Friedman comes close to suggesting, that if we can obtain the 'right' methodology then economics is more likely to arrive at results that are less ambiguous and therefore a new consensus could emerge. This hope is unlikely to be fulfilled from studying methodology. It will become apparent that no one methodology will rescue us from all our problems.

There are other writers who believe that the study of methodology could give rise to a new direction in economics. This group, in which I include myself, argue that the methodological biases of the past have restricted the ability of economists to deal with many of the problems of the late twentieth century. That is, economics has been modelled upon the natural sciences in a rather mechanistic fashion. This attempt to imitate the natural sciences is referred to as 'scientism' or 'naturalism'. It is my belief that if we view economics more as an organism then the methodological implications are quite radical. Therefore, although there is something to the crisis theory it does not completely explain why methodology has become more popular in recent years. Methodology is about very fundamental issues that go far beyond the whims of crises and fashion. The subject matters because the methodologies that different economists practice differ in subtle ways. If we are not aware of this, some of the nuances of their work can be lost.

What then is methodology? This is not an easy question to answer. Methodology means different things to different people. That this is so will become abundantly clear below. Although what methodology means is best dealt with in the more detailed context of each chapter, a broad outline will be presented here. It is concerned with the nature and status of a discipline. Methodologists typically seek to establish certain standards and criteria by which we can appraise and evaluate economic theories. In this context the notion of testability proves to be a primary concern in methodology and most of the chapters will consider the different ways in which this is approached. The appropriate balance between conceptual and statistical analysis has also been an important consideration within methodology.

As already indicated, the nature of economics has been moulded along the lines of the natural sciences. This is significant because it means that techniques designed for such sciences play an important role in economics and this applies particularly to the widespread use of mathematics and statistics. Methodology also needs to pay some attention as to how far such methods are appropriate to economics.

In writing this book I have two objectives in mind. When I studied methodology I found the lack of a clear and intelligible introductory book a great handicap. This feeling of frustration has heightened since I have taught my own methodology course. Consequently, my primary concern is to produce a book that will deal, in as simple a manner as possible, with a subject that is often rather difficult, and remote, to the unfamiliar reader.

My second aim is to present some arguments in support of those economists who see methodology as a useful means of promoting a different type of economics. This will be done by criticising the 'naturalism' of much economics and suggesting some of the alternative directions that can be taken.

In order to achieve these two objectives the book has been constructed in the following way. The first chapter deals with two extreme methodological positions, inductivism and deductivism. The former stresses observation and systematic statistical work as the best route to knowledge whilst the latter emphasises thought and introspection. Although few economists can be classified as fully fledged inductivists or deductivists there are two reasons why I begin my analysis with them. Firstly, many of the historical debates within economic methodology have been couched in these terms. Consequently it will be argued that they have left their mark on the approach adopted by many economists. Secondly, some of the other methodologies considered in the book are direct responses to, or elaborations upon, inductivism and deductivism. Therefore consideration of them serves a very useful scene-setting purpose.

The next chapter considers the work of Sir Karl Popper. His contribution has been largely stimulated by some of the issues arising from Chapter 1. We also appreciate the crucial signficance afforded to testability within methodological discussions. Chapter 3 deals with Thomas Kuhn. He has developed a more structural view of methodology which considers the way in which the scientific community sets and changes the standards of what counts as acceptable science.

The next two chapters, concerning Imre Lakatos and Larry Laudan, are in their own ways elaborations upon the methodologies of Chapters 2 and 3. The sixth chapter considers instrumentalism. This is a position that is derived from inductivism. I have postponed discussion of Friedman's famous essay 'The Methodology of Positive Economics' until this chapter for two reasons. Firstly, it will be argued that Friedman's essay is best interpreted as instrumentalist. Secondly, this methodological position is placed in a much clearer perspective when following the earlier chapters.

The Austrians form the subject of Chapter 7. They are a group of economists in the deductivist tradition who are typically suspicious of systematic statistical work by economists. We shall see that their rejection of 'naturalism' makes their position more interesting as well as more controversial.

In Chapter 8 I consider Marx's methodology: this is an approach that is both complex and difficult to categorise. The final section will consider some of the implications for treating economic methodology more as a vehicle for the study of an organic social science.

J.P

1 Inductivism and Deductivism in Economics

This chapter is concerned with two methodological positions, inductivism and deductivism, that have exerted some influence upon the methodology of economists. It should be emphasised immediately that I am not claiming that inductivism and deductivism are practised widely by a majority of economists. Indeed, my representation will be of a somewhat extreme variety of these two positions. However, I believe that consideration of them is helpful for two reasons: firstly, a number of the other methodologies discussed in this book were developed either as a reaction to, or development from, facets contained within inductivism and deductivism. Secondly, these two methodologies have done much to influence the general tone of economic methodology as something hard, rigorous and naturalistic. Consequently, they will hold important implications as to the type of economics we study.

The flavour of this chapter will be historical. However, limitations of space do not permit me to present a comprehensive discussion of the history of economic methodology. Anyone interested in pursuing this is advised to consult Blaug (1980), Caldwell (1982), Klant (1984) and Pribram (1983). My considerations will necessarily be limited to the more explicit manifestations of inductivism and deductivism within economics.

DEDUCTION AND INDUCTION

Before outlining inductivism and deductivism it is necessary to briefly consider the notions of deduction and induction. Deduction originally was, and still is, largely identified with logic and is a form of argument where we use the syllogism. The syllogism relates the premises of an argument to its conclusion. The following is an example:

(1) Premise: All men are mortal
     Premise: Keynes is a man
     Conclusion: *Therefore* Keynes is mortal

1

With this type of deductive reasoning we know that if all the premises
are true, and that we have not committed any of the fallacies of
deductive reasoning, then our conclusion will also be true. However,
logical arguments are not concerned with the truth or falsity of
conclusions, instead, such reasoning is interested in the correctness, or
validity, of the argument. Consequently, we could have a syllogism that
contains both a false premise and conclusion, but is valid in the sense
that the conclusion follows from the premises. For example, it is
unlikely that the following pertains:

   (2)   All demand functions are upwardly sloping
         There is a demand function for beer
         Therefore the demand function for beer is upwardly sloping

Conversely, inductive arguments may have true premises, but we can
never be certain that the conclusions derived from them will also be true:

   (3)   Swan No 100 is white
         Swan No 101 is white
         Therefore all swans are white

This conclusion is obviously false as we know that black swans can be
found in Australia. However, the example does highlight a notable
feature of inductive reasoning: it is *ampliative*. This is because the
conclusions drawn from such arguments go beyond the information
contained in the premises.

   From the above examples we can discern differences between
deduction and induction. Deductive arguments tend to move from
general to particular statements. In examples (1) and (2) we started with
general statements concerning the mortality of men and demand
functions and deduced the more particular statements relating to
Keynes' mortality and the demand function for beer. Induction involves
reasoning from particular statements towards more general ones.
Example (3) refers to two particular observations of white swans from
which we draw the more general inference that 'all swans are white'.
Although such clarifications are helpful we should be wary of drawing
too fine a distinction between induction and deduction. As Copi (1978,
p. 33) points out, the differences noted generally hold well. However, we
can devise syllogisms where deductive arguments may involve general
statements in both premises and conclusions, and inductive arguments
that contain general statements and conclude with a particular one. Also
the two methods, although different, should not be regarded, as some
economists appear to have believed, as being mutually exclusive.

INDUCTIVISM IN ECONOMICS

What I label as inductivism is a general approach that emphasises observation and systematic empirical work as being the major means of attaining knowledge. It should be emphasised that an important distinction needs to be drawn between inductivism and induction. Inductivism is a broad way of approaching scientific work; induction can and often does play an important part in this programme. However, the use of induction is a necessary but not sufficient condition to be an inductivist. Many economists happily employ induction, particularly in their statistical work, without feeling the need to embrace the complete inductivist package, which as we shall see, subordinates conceptual considerations.

Let us now consider the general methodological approach that we shall label inductivism. As this method is most closely associated with the work of Sir Francis Bacon in the early 1600s, we will outline his approach. Bacon was reacting to the authorities of the Church and Aristotelian deductive logic and he felt particularly strongly about the syllogistic and mathematical way in which deduction was practised. With the syllogism we can never get more out of our arguments than we feed in. Indeed, Bacon argued that many of the deductive philosophers tended to ponder on rather esoteric problems. They were too fond of 'spinning cobwebs of learning' with little practical result. Bacon wanted science to bear 'fruit' and help mankind generally. Some of the deductivist philosophers actually regarded attempts at rendering science more practical as immoral and degrading.

Bacon felt that the conservatism of the Church and deductive philosophy were not the only constraints. There were also the difficulties of our own tendencies to make rash generalisations and anticipate results before a full investigation had been undertaken. He argued that if we were open-minded and cautious in our approach then nature would be more likely to 'lay herself open to us'. This was not an easy task to accomplish. Bacon appreciated the significance of the so-called subject–object distinction. The object of our investigation could be nature. However, before any understanding of this object can be achieved, the subject (ourselves, as the investigators) needs to interact with it; there is a gap between subject and object that needs to be bridged and a fundamental methodological concern is to ensure that the interaction of the subject and object does not result in distorted results and conclusions.

With this in mind Bacon identified four Idols ('phantoms of the mind') that can interfere with our objectivity when studying nature. He wanted us to purge our minds of these Idols before undertaking any scientific work. The first three of these Idols we were normally unaware of: the Idol of the Tribe relates to our tendency to find an unwarrantable degree of order and regularity in the phenomena that we investigate. This stems particularly from our great desire to find uniformity in things. The second, the Idol of the Den, refers to the peculiarities of our individual characters that can interfere with our analyses. Such peculiarities are what we would today refer to as hang-ups, frustrations and neuroses. The Idol of the Market Place arises from the need, as social animals, to use a common language. The usage of words is often determined by fashions in society and this can result in our language possessing imprecise and ill-defined meanings that could hinder our efforts to develop science. The Idol of the Theatre, unlike the other three, is something that we are aware of and consciously develop. This Idol relates to the misleading information and analyses that we can associate with the dogmas that different schools of thought peddle. It is theatrical in the sense that each school produces a different representation of the imaginary world which they place at the centre of the stage.

Bacon wanted us to purge ourselves of such Idols before we began any systematic investigation. He wanted to ground scientific work in careful observation where we proceeded gradually, in a piecemeal fashion, from our particular observations towards the ultimate establishment of universal laws. It is clear that induction is to play a pivotal role in this. The role accorded to deduction was a very subordinate one.

By approaching our investigation with an open mind and not entertaining any expectations as to the likely results, we may be close to achieving objectivity and purging our minds of some of the Idols. Then we can begin our detailed observation and collection of facts. The primary objective at this stage of the enquiry is to propose a 'history' of 'all the phenomena to be explained'. This fact-gathering process needs to be very carefully conducted, with the facts being very thoroughly checked. After several years the assembly of such 'histories' would enable us to develop 'science'. Having established universal laws, theories and deduction then have a role to play. Bacon felt that until this stage was reached it was possible to divorce facts from theories.

Having completed the first stage, it is necessary to discover the 'Form' of the phenomena under investigation. The precise meaning of this term is not clear. It seems that 'Form' is likely to be synonymous with 'cause'. It is at this stage that Bacon's theory of induction is introduced to discover the 'Form'. Bacon adopted a type of induction known as eliminative, in contrast to another form, known as enumerative. Enumerative induction is where we gather together a number of particular, and similar, observations and draw some more general conclusion from them. Our example (3) of white swans is a case in point. If we had continued with that example and observed, say, 10 000 white swans then we might have been tempted to draw the conclusion that 'all swans are white'. Bacon recognised the dangers of such an approach. It is the differences, rather than the similarities, between particular observations that is often more telling. This is where eliminative induction proves helpful. Here we consider the phenomena that we are interested in under a variety of different circumstances in order to assess whether they affect it. If they do not, then we may eliminate such circumstances as having no direct bearing upon our observed regularity. Therefore, if we wish to check whether 'all swans are white' we may care to observe swans in different countries (as all native British swans are white), at different times of the year, their habits, etc. Such an approach, when checking on swans in Australia, would immediately render the generalisation false. Therefore, by eliminating factors that appear to have no direct bearing upon explaining the 'Form' we can move closer towards establishing the true cause of the phenomena that we are interested in.

Bacon believed that physics was 'the mother of all the sciences' and that his method could be applied to all sciences. Furthermore, he felt that we could ultimately determine the 'Form' of things with absolute certainty and with almost mechanical ease.

How feasible is such an approach likely to prove? Contemporary philosophers of science have tended to pour scorn on such an approach (see Chalmers, 1982; Hempel, 1966; and Medawar, 1969). The substance of their criticisms is as follows.

Chalmers strikes at the heart of some of the crucial features of the inductivist programme. We have seen how a more objective study can be undertaken once we have purged ourselves of the Idols: Chalmers, in effect, raises doubts as to the possibility of whether this can be achieved. He cites several examples where our viewing of an object is influenced by our previous knowledge, and expectations. One example is an experiment where people were asked to identify playing cards, after studying a pack for a short time. Generally, the subjects correctly identified the cards. However, when anomalous cards (for example, a red Ace of Spades) were introduced, the subjects encountered great difficulty in identifying them. They were influenced by their expectations and previous conceptions of playing cards. This, along with several other examples, leads Chalmers to argue that when we view things they are never impassive sense-data that register on our minds. Such images are strongly influenced by cultural background, anticipation and expectations.

Also, whenever we make an observation statement it is, by necessity, made in language that usually presupposes some theory. This is important because it implies the need for some theoretical construction *before* we can frame sufficiently precise observation statements for our empirical work. Therefore, the barring of all hypotheses, and the divorce between fact and theory, is untenable.

Hempel (1966, pp. 11–12) raises a number of questions regarding the practicality of adopting an inductivist procedure. Firstly, we could never collect 'all' the facts relating to the subject that we are interested in. He feels that this should more appropriately be 'all the relevant' facts. However, to what are they relevant? This would suggest that we have some problem, or tentative hypothesis, in mind to help shape what is relevant, but such devices are clearly ruled out in an inductivist programme at such an early stage of investigation.

A similar point can be made when we have to clarify and organise 'all' the facts. Let us imagine the way that we might choose to conduct a piece of economic research: I might be interested in the reasons for the West Midlands economy experiencing the highest rate of increase in unemployment in the UK between 1978 and 1982. Do I set out to interview and obtain information from 'all' the firms who are still in business or have gone bankrupt? Unless I wish to spend several years on such a task I am unlikely to adopt such an approach. Instead, I could resort to using some data that has already been gathered (by the West Midlands County Council), supplement this with some of my own questionnaire information and construct an input–output table. Having done this, by no means straightforward, task, I am in a position to check inter-industry linkages and multiplier effects. This enables me to form a clearer view of how the different sections of the West Midlands economy interrelate and which ones have particularly damaging multiplier feedback effects. It could be that my initial suspicions as to the traditional reliance of the West Midlands economy upon sectors vulnerable to import penetration and changing technology, such as the car, motorcycle, components, engineering and steel industries, is borne out. Now the approach I would have adopted would be anathema to any self-respecting inductivist. I am using a lot of secondary data, entertaining hypotheses and framing the input–output table in such a way that it fulfils certain theoretical requirements. Added to this there are some severe limitations associated with any construction of input–output tables. However, I would venture to suggest that in a few months I would have possibly obtained some useful insights into the problem of West Midlands unemployment before an inductivist has even interviewed his/her first 10 000 companies!

Medawar (1969, p. 40–1) raises some broader issues concerning inductivism. It does not provide us with an adequate theory of incentives. Why should we select to study one class of phenomena at the expense of some other? Failure to deal with such questions renders inductivism an unnecessarily restrictive method. Also we find that inductivists place too much emphasis on verification. This is not a straightforward business. Normally, scientific work encounters difficulties but rather than drop such work immediately we are more likely to adjust and refine it. Medawar also believes that insufficient scope is allowed by inductivists for the role that luck can play in the development of theories. Finally, he believes that experimentation should be used more for critical purposes than merely to generate information.

THE PROBLEM OF INDUCTION

The Problem of Induction is a difficulty that holds implications for empirical investigation generally, even for those who do not subscribe to an inductivist methodology. This problem was first raised by David Hume in the eighteenth century. He was pondering whether inductive evidence can go beyond the available evidence in order to predict future events. Past evidence, he argued, can tell us about past experience only. If we wish to go beyond this we are on dubious ground. He considered this (Hume, 1975, pp. 33–4) in relation to the nourishment he received from bread. In the past bread had nourished him, would it therefore continue to do so? The answer is not necessarily yes (especially if he contracted ergotism!). Hume's conception of this difficulty was cast in a very logical manner. He considered one way around the difficulty that could have been placed in the following syllogism:

> Bread has always nourished me in the past
> What has always obtained in the past will obtain in the future
> *Therefore* Bread will continue to nourish me

It is the second premise of the argument that raises problems. For it is effectively an appeal to the Principle of the Uniformity of Nature. This

states that a generalisation, or law, that has held in the past will continue
to do so. If this were the case we could justify inductive reasoning to
predict into the future. But can we? We cannot because appeals to the
Principle of the Uniformity of Nature result in us using an inductively
derived concept to justify induction. This is a circular argument and
therefore invalid. Consequently, the Problem of Induction arises from
our inability to provide rational grounds for using inductive inferences
that go beyond the evidence available. In a sense this is an unfair
criticism to make of induction, for it suggests that somehow we should
be applying the standards of deductive logic to induction. Induction is
not deduction and cannot be judged by deductive standards. The real
problem associated with the use of induction is not so much one of
rationality, but of reliability. This is troublesome because it is
impossible to know how reliable any of our inductions will prove to be.
Consequently, the 'control' that we hope to exercise over policy matters
that is frequently based on estimated macroeconomic relationships is
likely to be short-lived.

This problem does contain real implications for much of the statistical
and econometric work undertaken by economists. These issues were
perceptively considered by Mills (1924) in a piece that has not received
the attention it deserves. Mills fully appreciated the signficance of the
Problem of Induction for quantitative work in economics. He wanted
economists to face these difficulties and be aware of them, otherwise we
could easily be oblivious to the limitations of the techniques we employ.
He argued that our quantitative knowledge cannot be as concrete as that
of certain physical sciences. The knowledge we possess is of averages
and if we wish to go beyond this in order to comprehend ultimate causes
of the phenomena that we are interested in we enter the realm of
uncertainty. Consequently, probabilities and approximations are a
necessary part of economic reasoning. It is with such considerations in
mind that Mills distinguished between 'statistical description' and
'statistical induction'. The former relates to a particular class of
phenomena, or sample. Here the averages that we obtain are normally a
reliable representation of the phenomena contained in the sample being
studied. The latter is where we draw wider inferences based upon such
samples. It is with statistical induction that we encounter problems.
Mills writes:

> Quantitative inference of this type differs in no way from the ordinary
> process of induction, except in that one of the premises is in the
> quantitative form, and the conclusion asserts only a probable

connection, or extends an average value which may or may not hold in any given case. Both evidence and conclusion deal with only probable and approximate relationships or average values and in this respect accord more closely with actual experience, than do the premises and conclusions of universal induction.

The problem at issue in the discussion of the validity of the process relates to the reliability of the results, to the stability when applied beyond the sample, of the averages, rates or equations computed. The whole practical problem of statistics centres about the stability of such results, and the limits to such stability when the results are generalised in this way.

The factors in the case are practically the same as in the case of universal induction. Since we are generalising from a limited sample, some degree of probability must attach to the conclusion. To justify such a conclusion, moreover, an assumption about nature, similar to the assumption of uniformity suggested above must be made. . . . (Mills, 1924, p. 60)

Mills goes on to identify one such candidate, L. A. J. Quetelet's 'law of large numbers'. This is interesting because it provides the 'missing premise' that we need to render statistical induction 'rational'. Mills recognised that some such premise is essential if most statistically inductive techniques are to be rendered at all feasible. However, he warns that the probabilities obtained are empirical and therefore questionable. Mills warns that we need to interpret our results with care and modesty. This is sound advice that some may feel is unnecessary as it is 'obvious'.

Anyone believing this should read Mayer (1980); he points out a number of shortcomings of econometric practice. However, one point in particular that is interesting relates to the unreliable inductive leaps that so many econometricians still make. He refers to several studies where econometric relationships worked well during the sample period under consideration. However, when applying the same equation for post-sample periods they often performed badly. The problem was that often economists were not checking the later periods and were effectively claiming a degree of stability that did not exist. The Problem of Induction does throw considerable doubt about going beyond the evidence available and this has led some philosophers to adopt a position of scepticism with respect to the possibility of obtaining knowledge. It also helps to explain why the anti-empirical strains of deductivism have had so much influence within economics. However, a proper response to the Problem of Induction is to interpret our empirical results with care and never claim too much for them.

Despite the limitations associated with inductivism this methodology has had some influence upon the work of economists. In the early part of the seventeenth century William Petty was undertaking pioneering work in the collection of statistics in a way that owed much to the influence of Bacon. However, the first notably inductivist approach came from The Revd Richard Jones in the 1820s. As with Bacon, Jones was unhappy with the overly-deductive method that dominated economics at that time. Jones was particularly concerned with the abstract, axiomatic economics of David Ricardo, who used his theory of rent, Malthusian population theory and the assumption of diminishing returns in agriculture as axioms on which to build his conceptual model to analyse the distribution of factor shares. Jones was unhappy with the essentially axiomatic, non-empirical nature of Ricardo's system; he wanted economics to be far more factually based. Consequently, features such as Ricardo's theory of rent needed to be checked empirically. Otherwise an elegant and simple analytical system may be based upon very dubious foundations. He was also unhappy with the implicit 'universalism' of much Classical doctrine. He recognised that over time the institutional fabric of the economy changes and with it economic relationships.

Jones set out to check Ricardo's theory of rent by investigating *all* the systems and societies known to him. He discovered five different systems of rent throughout the world and from this he concluded that the universalism attributed to Ricardo's theory of rent was invalid. All this prompted Jones to endeavour recasting economics along very inductivist lines (see Hollander, 1983, pp. 138–9, for lengthy quotes to this effect). As Rashid (1979) points out, Jones was not a rigid inductivist; indeed, as Miller (1971, p. 204) notes, he was ultimately forced to employ deduction in order to bring his observations into some kind of order. Miller feels that Jones' attempts to demolish Ricardian method were also inappropriate. What was required was more the testing of the predictions of the model.

The concerns of Jones were also shared by the German Historical Schools of the mid- and late-nineteenth century. The two Schools of German Historicism have been labelled the Older and Younger. Although there were differences between them, such as to the notion and possibility of economic laws, they were agreed that economics needed to be far more empirically orientated. The Older school was generally agreed to have been founded by Wilhelm Roscher in 1843 and other important members included Bruno Hildebrand and Karl Knies.

Generally, they were as unhappy as Jones with the abstract and deductive nature of much classical economics, however, they differed in the way that they responded: Roscher was content in rendering classical doctrine more empirical by supplementing it with historical and empirical data; Hildebrand favoured a more radical approach that would render economics far more historically inclined (here the primary objective would be to investigate the laws of development of different countries); Knies wanted economics to adopt a more interdisciplinary approach. He expected different economies to exhibit alternative types and stages of development and this was to be treated as an evolutionary analysis where the particular forms of any economy would be strongly influenced by the type of social organisation prevailing.

However, the Older School never really established an alternative programme to that of the classical economists. This was left to members of the Younger School, the most notable member being Gustav Schmoller. When writing in the last quarter of the nineteenth century, he not only had the deductive method of the classicals to contend with, but that of the neo-classicals also. The deductive nature of the emerging marginal utility theory of value helped to give rise to the famous *Methodenstreit* (conflict of methods) between Carl Menger and Schmoller: the latter denied that there could ever be a law in economics that had not been empirically derived. Initially he advocated an approach where induction predominated. His basic view was that deduction was of little value in obtaining any understanding of the economy and that the historical method was the best way to proceed. By this he sought to follow a programme that was essentially inductivist. We would start by collecting vast amounts of historical information and see how it related to contemporary concerns. When this was done it would be possible for economists to derive, inductively, certain generalisations from such information. Such generalisations would form the basis of a useful practical comprehension of the economy that would be important for aiding the social reforms that Schmoller desired. He envisaged this process taking several decades to be completed. However, the demands on Schmoller to produce quicker results necessitated the use of more deductive forms of reasoning. By 1902 he conceded that induction and deduction were analogous to the right and left legs and that they were both essential for walking.

In this century other economists have advocated an inductivist programme. For example, one of the classic statements of inductivism came from the economist A. B. Wolfe. He suggested the following method for economists:

First, all facts would be observed and recorded, *without selection* or *a priori* guess as to their relative importance. Secondly, the observed and recorded facts would be analysed, compared, and classified *without hypothesis or postulates* other than those necessarily involved in the logic of thought. Third, from this analysis of the facts generalisations would be inductively drawn as to the relations, classificatory, or causal between them. Fourth, further research would be deductive as well as inductive employing inference from previously established generalisations. (Wolfe, 1924, p. 450 italics as in the original)

Chalmers and Hempel have made much of this quote as being an example of naïve inductivism. What they have not done is to be totally fair to Wolfe, for this classic statement of inductivism is followed by a series of qualifications and modifications that weakens the rigid view implied in it. For example, Wolfe recognises the frequent problem-orientated approach of much economic research and feels unhappy with the inductivist obsession with measurement.

Since then few economists have openly advocated an explicitly inductivist methodology. However, remnants of it still remain: McCloskey (1983) has labelled the methodology that economists purport to adhere to as 'modernism'. This is an interesting characterisation, because no single methodological perspective is dominant. Instead, several different aspects intermingle with each other. In this portrayal, McCloskey lists eleven features that we can identify with 'modernism' and what is interesting about this is that no fewer than six of these aspects possess a distinct inductivist flavour. We read, for example, of the importance given to objectivity and measurement. This attitude manifests itself in a widespread acceptance of Kelvin's Dictum, named after Lord Kelvin, who stated, 'when you cannot express it in numbers your knowledge is of a meagre and unsatisfactory kind'. Also 'modernism' seemingly frowns upon too heavy a reliance upon introspection and speculation that involves moral or value judgements. Furthermore, Boland (1982, p. 26) argues that we still encounter remnants of inductivism within economics. This manifests itself in the way economists treat hypotheses, theories and laws in a hierarchical fashion, as in the gradual inductivist search, from information that ultimately results in laws.

Positivism is descended from Bacon: here the expression 'positive' places the emphasis upon something that is clear-cut and definite. As a result, philosophical, metaphysical and theological thinking, although not dismissed as useless, are treated with suspicion by positivists – such areas of thought are likely to result in ambiguity and disagreement, which is to be avoided. For positivists, genuine knowledge is to be found within the confines of a systematic empirical study with a view to ultimately obtaining laws. Positivists were keen to be seen to set the standards of science as something hard and rigorous and, therefore, sound. Such sentiments proved very attractive to many economists (see Caldwell, 1982 for an excellent discussion of this).

Instrumentalism is another perspective that lays great emphasis upon systematic empirical work as the best means of avoiding tedious theoretical disputes. Instrumentalists are primarily interested in generating quantitative predictions in order to test their 'theories' (models would be a better expression). We shall see in Chapter 6 that this position has had some influence amongst economists.

Inductivism, therefore, seems to be more than a straw methodology. It helps to provide us with some helpful background for appreciating the sometimes sharp contrasts between those economists who favour a very empirical approach and those who do not.

DEDUCTIVISM IN ECONOMICS

My characterisation of deductivism requires some explanation. We have seen that deduction is primarily associated with syllogistic reasoning. However, to confine deduction to this would be as wrong as it would be unnecessarily restrictive. Deduction is an essential part in aiding our chains of reasoning and therefore in developing our conceptual analyses. Different economists emphasise different deductive devices. As will be seen in Chapter 7, many Austrian economists employ axioms as the foundation for their theoretical analysis. An axiom is a statement for which no proof is required; as a result it forms an important premise in an argument, but does not furnish us with a conclusion. More familiar examples of axiomatic reasoning are to be found in consumer behaviour. Axioms such as perfect rationality, transitivity and non-satiety enable us to derive indifference curves that are convex to the origin. This is important because this enables us to analyse maximisation problems of consumer behaviour.

An important complement to this type of deductive argument is the widespread use of mathematics. Indeed, this has probably become the main deductive tool within economics; it has also become one of the most criticised.

It should be stressed that there is an important distinction to be drawn between deductivism and deduction, analogous to the one already made between inductivism and induction. Deduction, whether axiomatic or mathematical, can be employed in a manner designed to facilitate, ultimately, statistical analysis and testing. However, deductivists believe that statistical and empirical knowledge is so transitory that it is largely worthless and that a primarily deductive analysis can provide greater understanding. Therefore we encounter a very distinct gulf between economists who lay much greater emphasis upon statistical work on the one hand, and those who stress reflection and introspection.

I shall begin my consideration of deductivism with the work of René Descartes, who in the early 1600s wanted to develop a new method that could release philosophy from the constraints of the orthodoxies of his time. He also devised this method to provide us with certain knowledge of all spheres of activity. Whilst the aims of Bacon and Descartes were similar, the means of achieving them were diametrically opposed. Descartes favoured the use of deduction and mathematics, techniques that Bacon had little time for.

Descartes began by doubting the adequacy of everything. This was significant because doubting become a crucial part of his method. He closely examined the premises of every argument and its conclusions until, by reason, such conclusions were as clear as they could be made and unless such arguments were absolutely convincing they would have to be rejected. This led him to doubt, at least initially, the existence of the external world and God. The only thing that he could feel certain existed was himself, as the doubting and thinking subject. From this he derived his famous phrase, *Cogito, ergo sum* (I think, therefore I am). This enabled him to arrive at some firm bedrock of certainty from which he could base his reasonings. This firm foundation was in his own consciousness. Consequently, the existence of the doubter is self-evident and can serve as the basis for the acquisition of all knowledge. Descartes developed this in the following way: as consciousness is the basis for all truth we need to look to it for clear replies to our reasonings, and if our consciousness declared something clearly, in response to our enquiry, then it is likely to be true. Descartes' fundamental axiom is that all clear and distinct conceptions are true. He proposed four rules that would enable us to detect such clear and distinct ideas. Firstly, we should not accept anything as being true unless we have no reason for doubt. Secondly, by the method of 'analysis' we should consider each question in terms of several separate questions. This would enable us to conceive of each part of the main question more easily. Thirdly, his notion of 'synthesis' was to begin by considering the most simple things and to progress towards analysing the more complex. Finally, we need to ensure that our analysis has not omitted any essential considerations. This part of Descartes' method rendered consciousness the basis of certitude. However he also needed to find a method for this certitude. This was to be found in the use and development of mathematics. He recognised that mathematics could be utilised to much greater effect by becoming simpler and more widely applied. His important role in the development of the relationship of algebra to geometry should not be lost on economists.

Consequently, deduction became a more flexible method and was no longer associated only with the syllogism. Syllogistic reasoning can be helpful for identifying the fallacies in our reasoning, but deduction took on new dimensions in the hands of Descartes: his method had no room for induction and the need for empirical verification. Indeed, Descartes criticised Bacon's approach for being liable to result in much 'superfluous' gathering of detail. This was due to our not having established *a priori* truths.

What do we make of this? One point that needs emphasising is that the basis of certitude that consciousness provides is fundamental to Descartes' system and if this is dubious then the whole structure will be found wanting. This does raise difficulties. I may be extremely clear in my consciousness as to ideas that are true, but what of others? The certitude that may be obtained from my own self-reflection cannot be extended to others. I may believe something to be so absolutely clear and true, but others may see things differently. Presumably Descartes desired general, as well as certain, knowledge. Therefore, where people disagree over something, some recourse to empirical verification may be necessary.

Descartes' method was also ambiguous regarding the important notions of clearness and distinction. It seems that he overcame this with a theory of Innate Ideas. Such ideas are truths that we necessarily hold independent of all experience. This is something that would be anathema to any inductivist.

In choosing Descartes as the main representative of deductivism it is worth noting that few economists have directly referred to him in their work. However the axiomatic nature of deduction that lends itself to mathematical manipulation, which he did much to encourage, has a strong tradition within economics. Recalling that Descartes did not favour systematic empirical work or induction we find such sentiments echoed by many economists. The view that there has been a significant

Cartesian tradition in economics is strongly shared by Dow (1985).

Initially, an important group of economists, the French Physiocrats, were strongly influenced by Descartes. Neill (1944) provides several quotations from Physiocratic writings which clearly display this preference for self-reflection whereby the fundamental principles of economics would become 'self-evident'. Characteristically, such sentiments were often accompanied by a rejection of the use of induction and empirical analysis. The deductivism of many of the Physiocrats, not entirely shared by their leading figure François Quesnay, sought to deduce all truth from Innate ideas. Indeed, they wanted to apply mathematics to political economy along similar lines to those taken by Descartes in philosophy. Hence, the development of a deductive and mathematical approach found many willing allies amongst the Physiocrats.

As noted above when considering the German Historical School, the classical economists have often been labelled 'deductivist'. However, this categorisation needs to be treated with some circumspection. Deductivism, in the sense defined here, is usually associated with a bias against induction and systematic empirical work. In this sense, we cannot label Adam Smith and Thomas Malthus as deductivists. Smith referred to the use of 'inductions' in his *Theory of Moral Sentiments*: in practice, his method is eclectic. He certainly employed deductive reasoning, but not of an axiomatic nature. He was a keen observer, of history and different societies and frequently used facts to illustrate his arguments. In short, his deductions were usually empirically founded. Therefore, we cannot say that Smith rejected or did not employ inductive arguments.

Malthus' views on economic methodology are less ambiguous. In the introduction to his *Principles of Political Economy* he appeals for a judicious use of both induction and deduction. Indeed the later editions of his *Essay on Population* are full of empirical findings designed to test his theory of population.

Of the leading classical economists, the arch-deductivist was David Ricardo. I have already referred to the essentially axiomatic, unempirical nature of his method which was quite intentional. In a revealing letter to Malthus, who persistently criticised his approach, Ricardo wrote:

> The second point is what is the practice? Now it is obvious that I need not be greatly solicitous about this latter point, it is sufficient for my

purposes if I can clearly demonstrate that the interest of the public is as I have stated it. It would be no answer to me to say that men were ignorant of the best and cheapest mode of conducting their business and paying their debts; because *that is a question of fact and not of science*, and might be used against almost every proposition in Political Economy. (Ricardo, 1952, p. 64, italics mine)

Ricardo regarded his abstract theorising as a useful means of unravelling the complexities of the economy. By employing 'strong cases' and 'self-evident' propositions he sought to arrive at principles that were 'as certain as the principle of gravitation'. This approach has been called, by Schumpeter (1954, p. 472), 'the Ricardian Vice', where we simplify and assume so many variables 'given' that the results of the model are predetermined and drop out almost as empty tautologies. The real vice is when the 'results' of such an analysis are applied to the real world and practical affairs.

Shortly after Ricardo, in 1836, Nassau Senior published his *Outline of Political Economy*, which contained an explicit advocacy of an axiomatic approach for economists. Senior felt that introspection and casual observation were sufficient to provide such an axiomatic basis. He considered four propositions to be 'self-evidently' true: firstly, every person wishes to obtain more wealth with as little effort as possible; secondly, the world population is limited only by certain moral and physical evils or by a fear of a drop in their living standards; thirdly, that the productive power of labour, and other 'instruments' which produce wealth, can be indefinitely increased by using their product as the means of further production; and fourthly, that the agricultural sector exhibits diminishing returns to scale.

Another notable piece of deductivist writing came with John Elliott Cairnes' *The Character and Logical Method of Political Economy*. This is a work that can be described as almost uncompromisingly deductive. Indeed, the book is essentially an attempt to defend the methodology and theories of Ricardo. Cairnes bemoaned the increasingly statistical character of economics where appeals were made more to results than to principles. He saw economics as representing the middle ground between mathematics, at one end, and the inductive natural sciences at the other. Economics resembled mechanics and astronomy where 'its premises represent positive facts; whilst its conclusions, like the conclusions of these sciences may or may not correspond to the realities of external nature, and therefore must be regarded as representing only hypothetical truth' (Cairnes, 1875, p. 48). He did not totally reject the use of induction, but it is accorded a very subordinate role in his scheme of things. Indeed for most purposes detailed inductive work was not required because:

> *The economist starts with a knowledge of ultimate causes.* He is already, at the outset of his enterprise, in the position which the physicist only attains after ages of laborious research . . . For the discovery of such premises no elaborate process of induction is needed. In order to know, e.g. why a farmer engages in the production of corn, why he cultivated his land up to a certain point, and why he does not cultivate it further, it is not necessary that we should derive our knowledge from a series of generalisations proceeding upwards from the statistics of corn and cultivation, to the mental feelings which stimulate the industry of the farmer on the one hand, and, on the other to the physical qualities of the soil on which productiveness of that soil depends. It is not necessary to do this – to resort to this circuitous process – for this reason, that we have, or may have if we choose to turn our attention to the subject, direct knowledge of these causes in our consciousness of what passes in our minds, and in the information which our senses convey, or at least are capable of conveying, to us of external facts. . . . (Cairnes, 1875, pp. 75–6, italics as in the original)

Indeed Cairnes adopted certain axioms that were very similar to those of Senior.

Although I have mentioned only three deductivists it is difficult to underestimate the influence that they exerted in Britain during the first three-quarters of the nineteenth century. Indeed, this helped to encourage something of a British *Methodenstreit* in the middle of the century when writers such as T. E. Cliffe Leslie, and later, J. K. Ingram and H. S. Foxwell wanted economics to pursue a more historical and inductive path (see Coats, 1954; and Koot, 1975, 1980).

Since the last quarter of the nineteenth century deductivism within economics has taken a different turn. The development of the marginal utility theory of value and general equilibrium analysis in the 1850s and 1870s held the key to introducing differential calculus and other mathematical techniques into economics. Despite the potential for the mathematisation of economics, the first mathematics text did not appear until 1924 with the publication of A. L. Bowley's *The Mathematical Groundwork of Economics*. New developments in economic theory in the 1930s, such as the development of indifference curve analysis and macroeconomics, provided further material for mathematically-minded economists to exploit. In 1947 Paul Samuelson's *Foundations of Economic Analysis* appeared, which introduced mathematical techniques to even more areas of economics. This book is still widely used on post-graduate programmes today and the use of mathematics within economics is now so widespread that it has become virtually impossible to read the major theoretical journals without a thorough training in mathematics.

Opinion as to the desirability of this more contemporary, and prevalent, form of deductivism is very sharply divided. Few would deny the value of mathematical manipulation for disentangling the complexities and intricacies of many economic models. Also the development of mathematical models can be an important step in the construction of models that are ultimately used for empirical work.

Granted that mathematics has an important role to play in economic analysis, there are many who believe that we have taken this too far. For example, Eichner *et al.* (1983) includes several contributions by economists who believe that the methodological problems facing economics are largely attributable to its overly-deductive nature, of which mathematics is a notable feature.

One of the contributors, Wiles, makes this point in no uncertain terms:

Without abstraction, as Friedman (and, indeed, nearly everybody) points out, one cannot handle the massive heterogeneity of economic data. But there is always a crucial level of abstraction; step above it and one's results are merely formal – too much has been left out for them to be credible or useful. Yet a high and useless level of abstraction has come to seem good in economics. . . . (Wiles, 1983, p. 69)

He continues

Then there are *axioms* (everyone maximizes his profit; resource allocation is the only economic problem); these are not known in other sciences. An axiom is only a premise one is not allowed to question, dressed up as something grand. But it is precisely the scientist's duty to question everything! Our crime is not that we use *a priori* reasoning, for often we can use nothing else, but that we push *a priori* all the way up to the axiom. 'Axiom' is, of course, a polite but impressive sounding word for a 'sacred proposition'. The concept gives us the impression that it is worthwhile to erect vast superstructures of deductions on virtually no fact, and this has now become a deep-rooted tradition. (p. 70)

He argues that the deductive devices adopted by economists represent our inheritence of the Ricardian Vice which helps to 'divert and corrupt our energies'.

Interestingly, Eichner (in Eichner *et al.* 1983, p. 207) identifies the way in which Descartes' test of coherence is still widely used today. This test involves ascertaining whether the consequences deduced are logically derived from the initial assumptions and whether such arguments are consistent. He feels that many economists, especially those favouring a highly mathematical approach, still regard this test as sufficient. It is partly because of this that Eichner argues that the basic propositions of neo-classical orthodoxy have never been empirically validated. However, the susceptibility of neo-classical orthodoxy to mathematical manipulation has played no small part in economists continuing to adhere widely to its foundations. Similar criticisms of an excessive use of mathematics are made by Hutchison (1984), Leontief (1983) and Prest (1983).

Other contributions within the Eichner volume include a professor of mathematics who raises several doubts about the way economists use mathematics, and others who feel that it is not enough simply to empirically test more of the mathematical formulations of economists. For the problem is often that economic 'theory' is either changed in order to accommodate mathematical manipulation, or the models are so unrealistic that no meaningful data exists, or they cannot be rendered empirically useful.

Inductivism and deductivism have affected economics in two main ways. Firstly, I believe that they have played some part in contributing to the split that exists between micro- and macroeconomics. This arises from their employing different ways of obtaining results, microeconomics being essentially deductive, whilst macroeconomics is more inductively inclined. This is no mere matter of differences in emphasis. As has been indicated above, the two approaches have very different ideas as to how knowledge can be acquired. Therefore, the two approaches will not always be compatible. A good example of this is the empirical testing of demand functions (for a good discussion of this see Green, 1976; and Koutsoyiannis, 1979). They argue that the theoretical conditions which make for a 'good' demand function are unlikely to be fully satisfied for empirical purposes. Consequently, what often happens is that statistical demand function estimation becomes a rather pragmatic exercise which pays little attention to theoretical niceties, indeed, those specialising in microeconomics have increasingly become involved in a field of study more akin to pure mathematics.

Macroeconomics, on the other hand, has long been viewed as the statisticians paradise, particularly since the 1930s. This area of study has been regarded as being particularly suitable for the deployment of the large-scale econometric models that have grown in sophistication since the Second World War. Just as an excessive mathematisation of economics can lead to 'theory without measurement' a number of critics have felt that macroeconomics has, to some extent, become an example of 'measurement without theory' (I will consider this latter point in more detail in Chapter 6). In so far as this is correct it is not surprising that economists have had so much difficulty in deriving suitable microfoundations for macroeconomics, for it seems that methodologically there are important incompatibilities between them.

The second way in which inductivism and deductivism have affected economic methodology is of a more general nature. It is no exaggeration to assert that the work of Bacon and Descartes has strongly influenced the way in which subsequent methodologies developed. Consequently, they have fundamentally influenced the standards by which science is largely judged. Economists felt compelled to comply with such standards and the result has been a heavy bias towards the study of economics that is both naturalistic and mechanistic.

2 Falsification and Economics

Sir Karl Popper's methodological writings have proved to be a source of much debate, and controversy, since the early 1930s and his views have received much attention from economists, many of whom support them. However, despite this interest in Popper's work it seems that a number of misconceptions are commonly encountered. For example, few economists seem to have fully appreciated the radicalism of Popper's approach. When we compare the practice of many economists against some of Popper's prescriptions we often find wide differences. More fundamentally, the more recent writings of Popper suggest that the methodology considered in this chapter was designed primarily for the natural sciences. Consequently, I shall need to consider not only the *feasibility* of Popper's method, but also its *applicability* to economics. In what follows I shall outline Popper's methodology, then evaluate it and consider how appropriate it is for economics.

The background to the development of Popper's views on methodology is detailed in his intellectual autobiography, *Unended Quest*, where we read about some of the significant events that influenced Popper during his formative years. A particularly important event that exerted a strong influence on his subsequent methodology, was his early flirtation with Marxism. He was very affected by a demonstration, organised by young socialists, which erupted into violence after a shooting incident. Eventually several demonstrators were shot dead by the Viennese police. Popper was not only horrified at the actions of the police, but also by his own complicity in the whole affair, for he felt that he was somehow partly responsible for the deaths of the demonstrators. This feeling stemmed from his short-lived commitment at that time to Marxism. He saw this as actively encouraging the class struggle and therefore in leading to the violent confrontation that had resulted in the deaths of the demonstrators. In so far as he was a Marxist, therefore, he felt some responsibility for these tragic events.

This had a profound affect upon him and prompted him to consider whether his belief in Marxism was justified. Was it scientific? Would it lead to a better world? Such questions troubled him for some time and his reaction after this period of intense self-reflection was to reject Marxism. He was disturbed by its dogmatic nature and more seriously, he was appalled at the way in which his own critical, and rational, faculties had been impaired by his adherence to Marxism. He felt that once you align yourself with a particular perspective it is too easy to ignore some of its limitations and inconsistencies; for Popper this was a serious 'intellectual sacrifice', because once one becomes committed to any cause one's intellectual integrity is easily compromised. Initially, Popper's doubts led him to react against rational thought and he even became a sceptic.

However, his soul-searching led him to draw certain conclusions that were to have a profound impact upon the methodology that he subsequently developed. He was unhappy with the way in which he and his friends had accepted a dogma; also the arrogance of believing that they had somehow acquired certain knowledge bothered him. From this his fallibilism (the view that our knowledge is never certain and therefore tentative) and his critical rationalism arose.

Also, during this time Popper had worked for the pyschiatrist Alfred Adler. One of Adler's theories relates to how human actions are motivated by feelings of inferiority. This theory is 'good' because it can seemingly explain all behaviour in certain circumstances. For example, both Chalmers (1982, p. 41) and Popper (1983, p. 169) cite the situation of a man who is standing by a dangerous river when a child falls in. The man may decide to save the child or not. If he does then an Adlerian would claim that the man overcame his inferiority complex by his brave action. If he does not jump in the Adlerian also has an explanation: in this case the man overcomes his feelings of inferiority by his strong will in remaining on the river bank as the child drowns. This example was something that Popper was very unhappy with as it is irrefutable; it was too 'good' as it explained too much. Popper felt the same way about some of Freud's theories (see Popper, 1983, p. 168).

In contrast to his views on Adler and Freud, Popper favoured the theory of relativity developed by Einstein. Now this theory, when brought to the test, was vulnerable. It could be falsified. This type of boldness in a theory excited Popper far more than those which explained away everything that contradicted them and the dogmatism that so often accompanied such theories became anathema to him.

He does not regard such dogmas as constituting science. This led him to formulate his famous demarcation criterion between science and pseudo-science. A theory that could not be falsified, where no restriction could be placed upon its applicability, was to be regarded as pseudo-scientific. However, that does not render it either metaphysical or useless.

POPPER'S ATTACK ON INDUCTION AND INDUCTIVISM

This demarcation criterion marked a radical departure from the prevailing view on methodology. This is because, for Popper, falsification is the direct antithesis of inductivism. With inductivism Popper saw the dangers of people seeking confirmations for a theory, or a set of beliefs, that they may cherish; this can easily result in an uncritical approach being adopted. Popper soon realised that the growth of knowledge was an important notion that was inextricably linked to his demarcation criterion. For the goal of the growth of knowledge is, in effect, the overturning of previous beliefs in order to arrive at better approximations to the truth.

As these thoughts crystallised Popper began to appreciate the radical implications contained within them. He began to realise that his attack was aimed at all forms of induction and inductivism. This attack is of a most uncompromising character. For example, he has stated: 'I go further than Hume. I hold that inductive procedures simply do not exist (not even low-level ones) and that the story of their existence is a myth' (Popper, 1983, p. 118). Why does Popper reject inductivism and induction in such categorical terms?

He raises several objections to Bacon's inductivism that we have already discussed. For example, he believes that most scientific inquiries begin with some problem in mind. Indeed he argues (Popper, 1972, p. 46) that the 'absurd' inductivist belief that we proceed from observation to theory is still widely encountered. Popper is not concerned with objectivity, at least in an inductivist sense. He believes that it is perfectly legitimate for us to frame whatever hypotheses and conjectures we like. This can even extend to 'silly' conjectures: the point is as long as we can test them, and potentially falsify them, the more ridiculous hypotheses are likely to be discarded promptly. This can smooth the way for more meaningful hypotheses to gain our critical attention. Objectivity, for Popper, arises more from a sincere attempt to adopt critical rationalism to our methods.

Popper proposes the following solution to the Problem of Induction:

> I happen to believe that in fact we *never* draw inductive inferences, or make use of what are now called 'inductive procedures'. Rather, we always discover regularities by the essentially different method of trial and error, of conjecture and refutation, or of learning from our mistakes; a method which makes the discovery of regularities much more interesting than Hume thought. The method of learning by trial

and error has, wrongly, been taken for a method of learning by repetition. 'Experience' is gained by learning from our mistakes, rather than by the accumulation or association of observations. It is gained by an actively critical approach: by the critical use of experiments and observations designed to help us to find where we have gone astray. (Popper, 1983, p. 35, italics as in the original)

Popper, when talking of induction, has both universal and numerical induction in mind. The former is where we expect a certain regularity to hold always, whereas the latter is restricted to holding for a shorter time period or confined to a narrower range of applicability. What is significant about this is that Popper regards attempts to employ inductive probabilities as being destined to failure. The reason for this is due to the situation of a universal induction. By its nature we expect events to occur continuously thereby giving rise to an infinity of observations. When we wish to obtain a probability from this we will be dividing by infinity. The result of this will be zero (Newton-Smith, 1981, pp. 49–50). This is quite devastating. Against probability theorists such as John Maynard Keynes and Rudolf Carnap, Popper is arguing that no amount of inductive evidence can raise the probability of any regularity above zero.

This radical attitude has resulted in Popper's proposal for the emphasis to be placed upon falsification. This is not unique to Popper. Others have found this concept helpful, but in Popper's hands it has been used very differently (see Agassi, 1969).

THE IMPORTANCE OF PROBLEM SOLVING

For Popper the search for truth and solution of problems is 'all important'. However he denies, unlike many inductivists and deductivists, that our knowledge can ever be certain: by necessity our ambitions should be more modest. Striving for certainty is likely to result in our falling into the bad habits of verificationism and, worse still, a dogmatic belief that we have discovered 'real' knowledge, hence his fallibilism.

How then does Popper recommend we proceed? The broad outline of his approach is neatly encapsulated in the following schema (Popper, 1976a, p. 132)

$$P_1 \longrightarrow TT \longrightarrow EE \longrightarrow P_2$$

The process begins with a problem. Popper requires that we provide a clear exposition of the problem and for this we can propose a tentative theory. Here hypotheses will be put forward which, it is hoped, can be tested and therefore have some bearing upon the problem under consideration. The next stage, error elimination, is crucial: this is where falsification is actively sought so that dubious hypotheses can be discarded. Inevitably the process is ongoing as fresh problems arise – this necessarily follows from Popper's belief that we can never arrive at ultimate truth; we strip off one layer only to continually discover yet another.

How do we go about this task and what qualities are required of us? A feature of crucial significance is the adherence to critical rationalism. By this Popper means anyone who is prepared to argue with others with a view to gaining a fuller understanding of the world. Argument does not mean heated controversy here. Rather it refers to a willingness to listen to, and act upon, criticism. Criticism is a fundamental aspect of Popper's methodology. He favours a situation where people disagree and sees widespread agreement as being unhealthy; indeed it is the very feature of theories being open to criticism that renders them scientific.

Virtually all criticism is intended to falsify theories. Popper feels that a theory can be critised both 'immanently' and 'transcendentally'. The first type of criticism is concerned with how well, or otherwise, any theory deals with the problem that it is designed to solve. Also if a theory deals with the problem less successfully than does a competitor this can also be treated as a source of criticism. The consistency of a theory is another important critical element. The second form of criticism is where we focus our attention specifically upon a competing theory to see how well it performs *vis-à-vis* our own theory.

Despite his fallibilism, Popper believes that critical discourse can be definite in one respect. Although truth may be ultimately unattainable, falsification can be clear-cut. If we can refute any theory this helps to clear the way for consideration of 'better' (by which Popper means those nearer the truth) hypotheses. His critical rationalism is also related to his realism as realists believe that there is an objective reality to the world waiting to be discovered. Furthermore, it is the case that there are certain theories that will help us to uncover the truth of this world. The difficulty is not only with discovering such true theories, but knowing that we have actually discovered them. Despite this acknowledged difficulty, Popper argues that criticism, in so far as it aids us in getting nearer to the truth, is a vital part of our intellectual equipment.

We see the significance again of the growth of knowledge, for this can be described as 'the critical review of our beliefs'. It is interesting to note that Popper feels that some degree of dogmatism is usually necessary to serve as a preliminary stage for the development of science. For it serves as a starting point from which criticism can be directed and lead to revisions. Although Popper dislikes dogmatism he later conceded a further role for it – he recognised that a new theory should not always be quickly refuted and that a degree of dogmatic attachment to it was legitimate in order to allow it to develop.

Critical rationalism is an important preliminary step in Popper's programme, but other concepts are required to take us beyond the situation outlined here:

> Critical reasons do not justify a theory, for the fact that one theory has so far withstood criticism better than another is no reason whatever for supposing that it is actually true. But although critical reasons can never justify a theory, they can be used to defend (but not justify) our *preference* for it: that is, our deciding to use it, rather than some, or all the other theories so far proposed. Such critical reasons do not of course prove that our preference is more than conjectural: we ought to give up our preference should new critical reasons speak against it, or should a promising new theory be proposed, demanding a renewal of the critical discussion. (Popper, 1983, p. 20, italics as in original)

The features needed to supplement this are Popper's concepts of the degrees of corroboration and verisimilitude (truthlikeness). The degree of corroboration for Popper is a qualitative rather than a quantitative guide to the acceptability of a theory. His rejection of inductive probability means that the tests of significance that economists employ are likely to prove unsuitable for his purposes. Positive degrees of corroboration can only be afforded to those theories that have not yet been falsified. Even greater degrees of corroboration will be assigned to those theories which are more vulnerable to falsification (such as those containing universal statements) and have managed to survive particularly severe tests.

Popper's more recently developed notion of the degree of verisimilitude is designed to complement the degree of corroboration by enabling us to consider, to some extent, how far unfalsified theories approximate the truth. The degree of verisimilitude is concerned with the balance between the truth and falsity contents of different theories. It is important to note that this concept can only be applied in situations where two or more theories are competitors and are covering broadly similar ground. Let us consider a very simplified, and unlikely, example. We may have two theories T_1 and T_2 that both contain five assertions. If we know that of these five assertions in T_1 three are false and two true, and in T_2 one is false and four true, then we may feel entitled to assign a greater degree of verisimilitude to T_2. More generally, we may have a situation where T_2 explains everything, and more, than T_1 and has also survived severe tests in areas where T_1 has little to say. In such circumstances we would regard T_2 as being of greater verisimilitude than T_1. Again the degree of verisimilitude is not a precise quantitative measure. Popper insists strongly that his degrees of corroboration and verisimilitude are in no way inductive.

METHODOLOGICAL RULES

All of the above is buttressed by the restrictions that Popper has sought to impose upon investigation. The rules proposed by Popper are analogous to the attempts of Bacon to purge us of the Idols. Popper seeks objectivity not in unbiased and unprejudiced observation where we forbid the entertainment of prior hypotheses and expectations; rather, he seeks to impose other constraints upon the subject (recalling the subject–object distinction) by offering guidelines and rules as to how we should conduct our scientific activity.

He feels that it is too easy to find confirmations, especially when we look for them. Consequently, confirmations can only count if they arise from a 'risky prediction', that is, we may well have expected many events to contradict our theory. There also needs to be a ban on what Popper has termed *ad hoc* adjustments to a theory that are designed solely to protect a theory from falsification. Rather than accept some falsifying evidence we may alter the content, or range of applicability, of a theory to protect it but such manoeuvres are generally to be avoided. An exception to this is where an adjustment increases the empirical content of a theory and renders it more vulnerable to falsification.

Some of the other rules have been detailed in Johansson (1975). He explicitly considers twenty such rules that appear in Popper's writings and argues that, implicitly, there are several others. Popper regards methodological rules as 'conventions' – in effect they are 'the rules of the game of empirical science'.

Some of the most important are:

1. The scientific nature of a theory is determined by its susceptibility to falsification.

2. If a refutation threatens a theory we should not rescue it by rendering it more resistant to falsification.
3. A new theory, in order to be acceptable, must always possess greater empirical content than its predecessors.
4. An acceptable new theory should be able to explain all the past successes of its predecessors.
5. Theories should always be tested as severely as possible.
6. Any theory which has been experimentally refuted should be rejected.
7. Any such refuted theory should not be revived at a later stage.
8. An inconsistent theory is unacceptable.
9. We should minimise the number of axioms that we employ.
10. Any new theory should be independently testable.

CRITICISMS OF POPPER'S APPROACH

How adequate is Popper's methodology? Having just referred to some of his methodological rules it is convenient to start by considering them. Several writers such as Feyerabend (1978), Johansson (1975), Lakatos (1978) and Maxwell (1972) have collectively argued that some of the above rules are more likely to hinder than promote scientific progress. They also believe that the rules are often too rigid.

For example, Maxwell focuses upon rules 3–8 above. Consider rule 3 – this is too severe. We are occasionally going to encounter new theories that possess, initially, less empirical content than rivals, but conceptually have much potential and such theories deserve our critical attention. Rule 4 also seems to demand too much; it ignores the fact that different economic theories focus upon alternative aspects of the economy. One theory, say Marxism for example, could accommodate business cycles and disequilibrium phenomena better than orthodox Keynesianism. Monetarists, in turn, would claim to possess a better explanation of the inflationary process than Keynesians. Keynesians might claim that their theory and policies would be most effective in combating unemployment. Consequently it is unlikely that the empirical phenomena explained by one economic perspective entirely overlaps with another, hence rendering Popper's notion of verisimilitude less useful.

Lakatos and Maxwell are particularly worried by 5. A new theory, when being developed, is often unlikely to be able to withstand the rigours of severe testing. Rather than reject it, we should nurture it and give it a chance to flourish. Take the example of Keynes' *General Theory*. He sought to explain why an advanced capitalist economy could experience sustained periods of high unemployment. This was something that other macroeconomic theories could not accommodate, much less explain. On conceptual grounds Keynes' theory was worth sticking with, a point on which Popper would probably agree. However, on empirical grounds there was little support for the *General Theory* initially. Keynes himself regarded the *General Theory* as a theoretical work and did not feel the need to engage in full-scale empirical work to test some of the hypotheses implied in it. Indeed there is evidence that Keynes wanted a period of 'gestation' to polish up the theory before it was empirically tested and used for policy purposes. Furthermore the development of more sophisticated econometric techniques after the Second World War rendered more meaningful tests of some of the *General Theory*'s hypotheses. However, this process took nearly twenty years. Therefore the rigid attempt to falsify new theories empirically can be damaging. Indeed what is more likely is that we will respond to difficulties by further articulating our theory.

What is ironic is that Popper has increasingly recognised the rigidity of such rules himself: 'Our scientific procedures are never based entirely on rules, guesses and hunches are always involved: we cannot remove from science the element of conjecture and risk' (Popper, 1983, p. 188).

A further difficulty for Popper's system concerns the so-called 'Duhem–Quine' thesis. This refers to the problem of devising crucial experiments that are so important for empirical falsifiability. Although we may be testing a particular hypothesis in effect we are dealing with a complex structure of initial conditions, auxiliary hypotheses and *ceteris paribus* clauses. Any hypothesis may be falsified experimentally but the basic theory may be sound. The falsification may be attributed to faulty laboratory equipment or an initial condition, necessary for the success of the theory, being unfulfilled (see Cross, 1982, for an interesting economic application).

Consider the example of Friedman's monetarism. He has stated quite categorically that increases in the rate of growth of the money supply are the only cause of inflation (Friedman, 1970, p. 24). This is a universal statement that is clearly vulnerable to falsification and furthermore Friedman has specified the relationship between changes in the rate of growth of the money supply and inflation. He has estimated that on average changes in the money supply affect prices between twelve and eighteen months later. Now this opens up the possibility of testing this particular monetarist hypothesis and this is something that is of particular interest as monetarist (or something like it) policies have become increasingly popular with governments recently. However the Duhem–Quine problem will immediately pose some difficulties: firstly, the lag of twelve to eighteen months itself is not regarded as in any way fixed, indeed Friedman has more recently spoken of lags stretching beyond two years. Also the length of the lag period will depend upon such initial conditions as the existing state of the economy and the way it is likely to respond to increases in the money supply. For example, the expected rate of inflation, the existing level of capacity utilisation and the rate at which unemployment is changing are features that Friedman has identified.

These types of considerations make it difficult to judge what the appropriate lag period between changes in the money supply and prices should be and in consequence statistical testing is rendered more difficult. This raises difficulties for those endeavouring to falsify theories empirically.

Indeed, we are likely to encounter a problem that is reminiscent of someone engaging in enumerative induction. Instead of asking how many positive observations we need before inductively verifying a relationship, we are asking how many falsifications does it take to falsify a theory? There is an obvious irony in this.

As a result it is possible that we may reject a theory by mistake. This is something that Popper recognises: 'All this, clearly, cannot absolutely prevent a miscarriage of justice; it may happen that we condemn an innocent hypothesis . . . an element of free choice and of decision is always involved in accepting a refutation, or in attributing it to one hypothesis rather than to another' (Popper, 1983, p. 188). This is analogous to what we term Type I and Type II errors in statistical testing. A Type I error is where we reject a true hypothesis and a Type II error is where we accept a false one.

Such considerations, which arise from the Duhem–Quine problem, can easily render the border line between *ad hoc* manipulations and genuine reluctance to accept a questionable 'falsification' a thin, if not precarious one. Who is to say that Friedman is not perfectly entitled to argue that his monetary theory remains intact, especially if mismanagement of the policy and 'awkward' initial conditions pose problems?

Popper has responded to such problems by re-emphasising (Popper, 1983, pp. xx–xxv) the important distinction between logical and empirical falsifiability. Logical falsifiability relates to the existence, in principle, of potential falsifiers; empirical falsifiability refers to the truth, in practice, of a falsification. Popper has sought to argue that the admittedly difficult problems of empirical falsifiability 'should not be taken too seriously'. Is there a whiff of *ad hoc* manipulation here? The reason I pose this question is that Popper clearly devises his methodology to act as an encouragement to empirical science. Although his purely logical notion of falsifiability may be 'untouched', this limits the applicability of his methodology for many of the more practical purposes that economists are interested in. It is certainly the case that many economists have, understandably, chosen to emphasise the empirical nature of falsification.

Another criticism that has been levelled at Popper is that he is not successful in his attempt to dispense with induction. O'Hear (1980, pp. 62-7) makes some telling observations. He points out that Popper has effectively conceded that there is an essential need to adopt inductive assumptions about the world in order to render knowledge of it intelligible. It seems that Popper accepts that something like a Principle of the Uniformity of Nature is necessary for us to observe a world of continuing regularities where the acquisition of knowledge is made far easier. Putnam (1981, p. 63) compares and contrasts an inductivist way of testing theories with Popper's attempts to falsify and obtain greater degrees of corroboration and concludes that there is little difference between the two approaches. Furthermore, the implicit inductive nature of the degrees of corroboration and verisimilitude is well-developed by Newton-Smith (1981, pp. 67-70).

POPPER AND ECONOMICS

Popper's work has increasingly played a part in methodological debates within economics. This has especially been the case since the late 1950s when his *Logik der Forschung* (Logic of Scientific Discovery) was first translated into English.

In this section I shall consider some of the economic methodologists, economists and econometricians who have found Popper's perspective attractive. I shall then consider, more generally, whether economists actually practise any of Popper's prescriptions. This will lead me on to a consideration of the appropriateness of Popper's methodology for economists.

From what has been stated above it is clear that for practical purposes Popper's position is far from ideal. It seems that many economic methodologists have, implicitly or explicitly, recognised this.

Consequently, we often encounter somewhat diluted versions of Popper.

Take the example of T. W. Hutchison's *The Significance and Basic Postulates of Economic Theory*, first published in 1938. This was one of the earliest attempts to apply a Popperian framework to economics. Hutchison had spent some time in Germany during the 1930s and was alarmed by the rise of totalitarianism that he was witnessing. On reading Popper he obviously encountered a kindred spirit. Hutchison was also unhappy with the overly axiomatic and deductive nature of much economic method of that era. This led him to propose a demarcation criterion that owed much to Popper (see Hutchison, 1960, pp. 26–7). One of Hutchison's main objectives was to steer economics along a more empirical line. Although there is a Popperian note struck in his writings he was probably more deeply influenced by the positivists, especially Moritz Schlick. Now Popper does not regard the positivists very highly, but despite this he has remarked favourably upon Hutchison's methodological writings (see Popper, 1976a, p. 127). What is interesting about Hutchison's falsificationist/positivistic tendencies is that they ruffled quite a few methodological feathers within the economics profession. More deductively-inclined economists, such as Lionel Robbins and Fritz Machlup, were not very taken by the 'ultra-empiricism' advocated by Hutchison (see Caldwell, 1982, chs 6 and 7 for a full discussion of this interesting episode).

More recently, other economists have considered the applicability of Popper's methodology for economists: Mark Blaug (1976, p. 149) has argued that Friedman is 'Popper-with-a-twist applied to economics'. By this he implies that Popper has had a significant indirect effect upon economists – this arises from the pervasive influence of Friedman's methodological writings which Blaug feels owe something to Popper.

In his more recent methodological work, Blaug (1980) takes a very strong falsificationist stance. He is of the opinion that contemporary economists are happier to preach falsificationism than to practise it. Indeed he goes so far (see Blaug, 1980, p. 254) as to argue that the unwillingness of economists to develop theories 'that yield unambiguous refutable implications, followed by a general unwillingness to confront these implications with the facts' is the 'central weakness' of modern economics. These are interesting comments. I shall shortly agree with Blaug on the first point, but on the second point I differ as it is less than certain whether falsificationism is the most appropriate approach to adopt. In his book Blaug perceptively considers many of the limitations and ambiguities that can be associated with Popper's methodology, but still argues strongly for it. This is more puzzling when we realise that Blaug employs a Lakatosian methodology in the latter part of his book. We have already seen how Imre Lakatos found Popper's system too restrictive; he recognised that theories often required protection and a greater degree of flexibility. It will, in fact, become apparent in Chapter 4 how far Lakatos has departed from Popper.

Why then does Blaug insist so much on falsifiability? Hands (1984) raises similar points to those just made: he believes that Blaug's insistence on falsifiability is motivated by fear; and he feels that Blaug wants to keep the 'riff-raff' out of economics (by this he seems to mean groups of economists whose theories are difficult to test and therefore border on being pseudo-scientific). However, the problem with this, as Hands notes, is that an aggressive attempt at falsification would almost certainly bring with it casualties. You may get rid of the 'riff-raff', but some useful theories may also bite the dust in the process. Here Hands also employs the Type I and Type II error analogy that I used earlier. This serves to emphasise the important point raised above that a strong adherence to Popperian methods can, and is likely to, retard or prevent progress within economics.

Boland (1982) provides another example of a writer who is attracted to Popper. He also recognises that many economists, despite indications to the contrary, do not practice Popperian methods. He believes that Popper's main accomplishment within economics has been to deter any open advocacy of inductivism. Boland realises that many propositions within economics are unfalsifiable, for example, the maximisation postulate. What is interesting about Boland's treatment of Popper is that he argues that issues such as those of demarcation and the growth of knowledge are non-issues and have led to much fruitless controversy. The rejection of such fundamental aspects of Popper's methodology signals a significant departure from the outline presented in this chapter. However, Boland has recognised the importance of methodological individualism to both economics and Popper and I shall return to this point shortly.

Other methodologists have cast doubt upon the feasibility of Popper's approach. Amongst these we can include Caldwell (1982, pp. 124–8), Hindess (1977, ch. 6) and most significant, perhaps, Klant (1984) – his is an extremely detailed attempt to assess whether many areas of economics can fulfil the demands made by Popper. Generally, he argues that economics is unable to comply with the requirements of falsifiability and severe testing.

Attention to Popper's work has not been confined to economic methodologists. Increasingly, economic journals are containing references to his writings, also some very well-known economists have endorsed Popper's work. For example, R. G. Lipsey, in his popular textbook *An Introduction to Positive Economics*, contains an introductory chapter which owes something to Popper:

> Thus if we really want to give a pet theory a run for its money, to show that it is a good theory, then we should not ask 'Can we find a lot of facts which agree with the theory?' seeking thereby to confirm it (it would be a pretty measly theory if we could not find some facts which agreed with it), but rather we should ask what tests would expose the theory to a serious chance of being refuted. The more critical is the test, the greater will be our satisfaction if our theory passes the test. (Lipsey, 1963, p. 14)

Lipsey's position at that time reflected the early wave of interest in Popper's work. However, despite an open acknowledgement of the influence of Popper, Lipsey's own position has undergone gradual changes as his book has passed through different editions. Presently we are into the sixth (1983) edition of his book. What is interesting is that here Popper is no longer mentioned.

More recently, Friedman has claimed some affinity with Popper (see Boland, 1982, p. 171). I shall argue that Friedman's position seems closer to instrumentalism which, as we saw in the last chapter, is derived from inductivism. In so far as it is, it is therefore strange to claim any affinity with Popper. I shall have more to say about this in Chapter 6. Robbins (1971, p. 41; 1981) was also impressed by Popper's work. Renewed calls to adopt something like a Popperian position have also come from Rutherford (1984) and Loasby (1984).

Econometricians have also paid some attention to Popper. Hendry (1980) feels that econometric practice is consistent with the falsificationist tradition. This is very doubtful: as Pesaran and Smith (1985) point out, technical considerations effectively render most econometric results difficult to falsify. Added to this, such considerations ignore the inductive foundations of much of the statistical work undertaken by economists. Indeed Popper (1976b, p. 143) has remarked upon the difficulty of undertaking statistical work within economics.

It is difficult to avoid the suspicion that many economists have failed to appreciate fully the implications and radicalism of Popper's method. The plain fact is that the majority of economists seek to verify, rather than to falsify their theories. This is well illustrated in a study undertaken by Canterbury and Burkhardt (1983) in which they studied

542 empirical articles that appeared in the *American Economic Review, Journal of Political Economy, Quarterly Journal of Economics* and *Economic Journal* between 1973 and 1978. Their results showed that only three of these articles attempted to falsify the hypotheses being tested. They concluded that there appears to be little attempt on the part of economists to falsify positions that they hold dear. Mayer (1980) complains that journals lay too much emphasis upon accepting articles for publication which verify hypotheses. He believes that this contributes to a number of dubious practices designed to obtain 'good' results. As he writes, 'if you torture the data long enough they will confess'.

Also it will be argued in the next chapter that economists, both consciously and unconsciously, appear to find the approach of Thomas Kuhn more convivial. This is significant because it will provide further indications that economists behave in un-Popperian ways. This should not necessarily be taken as a rebuke to economists, as Popper's position does seem to be less helpful than it first appeared. In his attempts to glamorise science and present it as a bold and enterprising activity he has overlooked the fact, as Kuhn observed, that the majority of scientific work is rather humdrum and routine.

Finally, it is becoming clear that Popper's methodological prescriptions were not formulated with a *social* subject matter in mind (Popper, 1983, p. 7). Rather it is the approach of methodological individualism (see Chapter 7) that Popper seeks to promote for the social sciences. It seems that a lot of heated controversy over a questionable methodology could have been largely avoided!

3 Kuhn and Economics

The work of Thomas Kuhn, an historian of science, has generated much interest amongst economists since the publication of his *The Structure of Scientific Revolutions* in 1962. Kuhn's work has been interpreted as a direct response to both inductivism and falsificationism and he is certainly opposed to the former. However, whilst *The Structure of Scientific Revolutions* was not intended to be an explicit response to Popper it can be, and has been, interpreted as such; indeed, we shall see that Popper interprets it in this light. It will become evident that there are notable differences between them; I shall outline Kuhn's schema of science and evaluate it, then I shall consider how applicable his approach is to economics.

Kuhn rejects totally the orthodox inductivist view of methodology. He does not regard science as an individualistic, piecemeal or incremental process. Rather, science is dependent upon adopting a particular view of the world and subsequent research activity will be designed to fit the facts into this preconceived view. Kuhn argues that until any science adopts a reasonably unified view of the phenomena with which it is interested, little, if any, progress can be made.

Kuhn considers different stages through which scientific development is likely to pass. Pre-science is a situation where there are several theories competing with each other to explain similar phenomena and research will frequently be in some disarray. It will be analogous to the situation of the naïve inductivist who eschews the use of a conceptual framework, and as a result facts will be gathered without reference to anything in particular. This can present us with the awkward situation where all facts appear to be equally relevant. Consequently, scientists, at an early stage of development, in confronting broadly similar phenomena will interpret them in very different ways. Kuhn does not regard this pre-scientific stage as being very conducive to progress – this will not be achieved until the scientific community has established a greater degree of order and coherence in its activities.

THE PARADIGM

This is greatly aided by Kuhn's important notion of the paradigm. There are two features of paradigms that are particularly notable: firstly, it

37

signifies an achievement that is considered so important that it attracts an 'enduring group' of adherents away from competing modes of scientific activity; secondly, such a development leaves unresolved a sufficiently large number of problems for these new adherents to research into.

The significance of the paradigm is well illustrated by Kuhn when he writes:

> The study of paradigms . . . is what mainly prepares the student for membership in the particular scientific community with which he will later practice. Because he then joins men who learned the bases of their field from the same concrete models, his subsequent practice will seldom invoke overt disagreement over fundamentals. Men whose research is based on shared paradigms are committed to the same rules and standards for scientific practice. That commitment and the apparent consensus are prerequisites for normal science, i.e. for the genesis and continuation of a particular research tradition. (Kuhn, 1970a, pp. 10–11)

Kuhn feels that the acquisition of a paradigm and the more esoteric research it facilitates is a sign of maturity, for without a paradigm it is difficult to discriminate between facts that are relevant to one's concerns. Fact-gathering can easily become a tedious hit-and-miss affair that often relies heavily upon the sources of data at hand. However, with a paradigm as a guide, useful and relevant information can more easily be obtained.

Kuhn sees new paradigms being accepted more readily by the younger generation, and members of the older generation who cling on to an older paradigm in the face of criticism that appeals to the majority of the young, are likely to find their influence fade. The paradigm also has the advantage of releasing scientists from the need to engage in debates over fundamental assumptions – such functions can be achieved by textbooks. Scientists can then concentrate on the 'subtlest' and more 'esoteric' aspects of the phenomena that interests the group, therefore a paradigm can be viewed as a guide to a whole group's research.

Paradigms are not presented to us 'ready-made'; it is usually the case that their scope is initially limited. However, the status of the paradigm will be enhanced when it is seen to be able to cope more successfully, than will competing perspectives, with problems that the group regard as important and generally further articulation and clearer specification will accompany the development of a paradigm. This process of articulation does not necessarily involve the search for universal laws;

Kuhn argues that 'statistical' laws are also likely to prove of great significance.

NORMAL SCIENCE

The notion of the paradigm sets the scene for the next important stage of Kuhn's schema: that of normal science. The concepts of paradigm and normal science are virtually synonymous, however, normal science constitutes the 'actualisation' of the promise provided by the paradigm. This actualisation is 'achieved by extending the knowledge of those facts that the paradigm displays as particularly revealing by increasing the extent of the match between those facts and the paradigm's predictions and by further articulation of the paradigm itself' (Kuhn, 1970a, p. 24). Indeed, normal science can be equated with the 'mopping-up' work left by a paradigm and Kuhn regards this as the typical work of most scientists. The main purpose of normal science is to 'force nature into the preformed and relatively inflexible box that the paradigm supplies'; it is not the purpose of normal science to bring forth new discoveries. Indeed, phenomena that do not fit into the paradigm are unlikely to be 'seen', and furthermore, most scientists are not keen to invent fundamental new theories and are intolerent of those who attempt to do so.

The 'mopping-up' work is largely concerned with 'puzzle-solving'. This activity, within a normal scientific tradition, will normally encounter three classes of problems:

(i)   the determination of significant facts;
(ii) the matching of facts with theory;
(iii) the articulation of the theory.

The work of all scientists operating within a particular field will inevitably fall into one of these categories. Kuhn argues that 'work under the paradigm can be conducted in no other way, and to desert the paradigm is to cease practising the science it defines' (Kuhn, 1970a, p. 34).

All experiments within normal science can only be conducted within the confines of a particular paradigm. In fact, most scientists are likely to suspect the results of their experiments before conducting them:

> Though its outcome can be anticipated, often in detail so great that what remains to be known is itself uninteresting, the way to achieve

the outcome remains very much in doubt. Bringing a normal research problem to a conclusion is achieving the anticipated in a new way, and it requires the solution of all sorts of complex instrumental, conceptual and mathematical puzzles. The man who succeeds proves himself an expert puzzle-solver, and the challenge of the puzzle is an important part of what usually drives him on. (Kuhn, 1970a, p. 36)

Puzzle-solving, as an activity, is not designed to test the paradigm, for this is usually taken for granted. Indeed, when a puzzle is unsolved the blame is initially directed at the aspiring puzzle-solver. That person's competence to deal with the puzzle is what is immediately questioned. Normal science imposes standards, and expectations, that effectively test the skills of the scientist.

THE PROCESS OF CHANGE

So far I have only considered the situation where normal scientific activity has emerged from a 'pre-scientific' state and this is, of course, not always the case. For Kuhn's schema seeks to deal with developments in established sciences and this raises the question as to what serves as the impetus for discovery and development? A preliminary feature of this process occurs when we encounter 'anomalies' in both fact and theory.

Fresh discovery begins when anomalies arise. The significance of anomalies is that our 'paradigm-induced expectations' of the world are violated and initially this leads to a concentration of work effort within the anomaly area, which may result in an adjustment being made to the paradigm's theories. Kuhn sees such adjustments as being more than mere increments to the existing paradigm. Indeed, until we have modified our view of the world to accommodate any new fact it cannot be regarded as scientific. All new phenomena will not be treated with equal interest or significance – this depends on how seriously our paradigm-induced expectations are considered to have been violated by the scientific community. The role of anomalies is often to prepare the way for discovery, but such discovery emerges 'only with difficulty, manifested by resistance against a background provided by expectations'.

An anomaly may not always be accommodated within the paradigm and the anomalous difficulty may, in such cases, begin to pose a threat to the paradigm. Where an anomaly has not been dealt with to the satisfaction of the majority within the scientific community a crisis situation may develop and this situation encourages a proliferation of competing theories and explanations to be developed. Crises typically 'blur' the sharpness of a paradigm, so Kuhn envisages three possible responses to this:

1. Normal science may ultimately prove capable of dealing with the crisis-provoking problem.
2. Sometimes the problem will resist new approaches to find a solution. Therefore scientists may put it 'on ice' and leave it for future generations to deal with.
3. A crisis may result in the emergence of a new candidate for paradigm and an ensuing battle.

The last possibility may result in a period of extraordinary science where much attention is focused upon the problem area. It has been suggested that during such an episode some attempt may be made to falsify the paradigm, but Kuhn does not accept this. If difficulties become severe the ultimate rejection of one paradigm will result in the acceptance of an alternative, therefore what is usually involved is the verification of an alternative paradigm. This is important for Kuhn because if we do not have another paradigm to replace the troubled one this is tantamount to a rejection of science.

The transition from one paradigm to another is not achieved by tinkering at the edges; what is involved is a fundamental change in the basic theories within a certain field. Also many 'elementary theoretical generalisations' and methods associated with the old paradigm are dispensed with: in short, although the world has not changed, our view of it has.

Philosophical reflections tend to be placed in the background during reasonably successful periods of normal science and the need for explicit rules and assumptions is often felt to be unnecessary. However, this changes during a period of crisis when fundamental assumptions are examined and more philosophical, and methodological, reflection is undertaken.

REVOLUTIONS

When the crisis has deepened, the stage is set for revolution. Revolutions are characterised by the following features:

1. They are necessitated by the rejection of an established theory for one that is incompatible with it.
2. This leads to further changes in the problems available for consideration and the standards by which they are assessed and regarded as solved.
3. The paradigm shift entailed during such a period brings with it nothing less than a change of the 'world view' of the scientific community.

The revolution will be very decisive. Basically, newly-established paradigms destroy old ones and much of the theory associated with old paradigms will be considered redundant. The old and new paradigms will necessarily be incompatible because the new paradigm, in order to be acceptable, must make novel predictions and deal with problems that the old paradigm could not cope with. Indeed, the upholders of two different paradigms are likely to be 'at least slightly at cross purposes'. Also, neither side is likely to agree with the non-empirical assumptions that their opponents make – the competition cannot be resolved with the certainty of proofs. This helps to render alternative paradigms incommensurable, and therefore difficult to compare directly. There will always be an element of a 'conversion experience' involved in the shift from one paradigm to another, also the new paradigm will displace the old one.

The successful close of a revolution will result in total victory for one paradigm. During a revolutionary stage we are likely to encounter attempts to rescue ailing paradigms in an *ad hoc* manner, similar to that identified by Popper (Kuhn, 1970a, p. 100). When a paradigm shift occurs it is not legitimate to argue that a particular methodology has been replaced by a superior one. Methodologies are peculiar, and appropriate, to the paradigms they serve. Consequently, a methodology associated with a displaced paradigm may well have been excellent for that paradigm's purpose; it will be the new paradigm that is superior. Any paradigm defines the *scope* of research activity and the methodology associated with it is but one, admittedly important, constituent of that paradigm. In Kuhn's writings he seems to be tolerant of different methodological perspectives, apart from falsificationism and inductivism.

Kuhn regards revolutions as occurring 'frequently in science' and being 'fundamental to its advance'. However, there is one feature of revolutions that he is unhappy about: this concerns textbooks and the distorted view of the history of science which they often convey. They typically portray the 'stable outcome' of previous revolutions from the standpoint of the current normal scientific tradition. He feels that this often results in the treatment of history being 'systematically misleading'. Textbooks have to be rewritten in order to propagate the prevailing normal scientific tradition, indeed once a textbook appears it is almost as if nothing has happened. Often the very existence of the revolution is scarcely mentioned or, at best, disguised and this can lead to serious misunderstandings of the history of a discipline. We can often be left with the impression of belonging to some well-established tradition, which can be compounded by the very selective way in which the history of a subject is treated. For example, an absolutist approach towards the history of a discipline is frequently encountered. This is where we tend to judge past theories by contemporary standards and it can result in our ascribing to earlier writers the view that they were somehow concerned with similar problems to the ones that engage us. This helps to reinforce the impression that science is essentially cumulative.

THE APPLICABILITY OF KUHN TO ECONOMICS

The above scheme has been employed by economists in two ways. Firstly, the scheme has proved interesting to historians of economic thought and the structure of scientific revolutions has provided them with a sharper focus for some of their work. I will consider some of this shortly. Secondly, Kuhn considers his concept of normal science as being 'intrinsically sociological'. This is because we are interested in the group behaviour of the scientific community and the implications that this holds for their activities.

Let us now consider how feasible Kuhn's approach is likely to prove for economics. I shall consider some of the criticisms that have been made of Kuhn and their implications for economics as the concept or, more accurately, concepts of the paradigm have come in for much criticism. Masterman (1970) has identified twenty-two different senses in which Kuhn uses the word 'paradigm', while Shapere (1971) feels that such looseness of definition of the paradigm enables it to cover 'anything and everything and allows the scientists to do anything', that is, we could say that science is what scientists do! Kuhn's insistence that we cannot precisely define a paradigm renders more likely such ambiguities as to what scientists do. This is because paradigms are often 'implicit' and are never fully articulated. Shapere argues that the vagueness surrounding Kuhn's definitions of a paradigm serves to blur the distinction between normal and revolutionary science, and this renders the distinction between them one more of degree than of kind. Some economists have made precisely the same point. Bronfenbrenner (1971) believes that in economics we rarely have one paradigm completely replacing another. What we experience is a synthesis emerging between different perspectives; this means that both continuity and discontinuity can be features of the history of economics. Kunin and Weaver (1971) develop this by pointing out that the level of generality at which we define a paradigm is significant. They suggest that different paradigms are more or less general and abstract. Once we recognise this it helps to explain why economists differ as to the number of revolutions that we have experienced. A more ambitious paradigm may fall more easily than a more specific one and we might talk of the occurrence of a revolution. Kunin and Weaver also make the point that in economics, unlike the world of physics considered by Kuhn, the institutions and structure of the economy, and not merely our view of them, *do* change. Consequently, the analysis of paradigm change is rendered more subtle and complex in economics. Stigler (1969) reiterates some of the doubts concerning the loose definition of paradigms. He believes that it seriously limits the applicability of Kuhn's schema to the study of economics.

Laudan (1977, pp. 74–6) has raised other doubts concerning paradigms. He believes that Kuhn does not appreciate the significance of conceptual problems and the role they play in paradigm evaluation. What connection do conceptual problems have with progress? Laudan argues that is unanswered by Kuhn. He also raises the issue of the relationship between a paradigm and the theories that constitute it: is it the case that the paradigm entails, or inspires, such theories? Or, when developed, do the theories justify the paradigm or vice versa? Laudan feels that Kuhn's treatment of such issues is inadequate.

Laudan also points to what he sees as a paradox with paradigms. He argues that the very rigidity of a paradigm's structure will often not permit it to respond to the difficulties and anomalies that it spawns. Furthermore, by rendering the basic assumptions of a paradigm irrefutable, by definition, there is no corrective mechanism operating between the data and the paradigm. As a result, Laudan believes that it is difficult to reconcile the inflexibility of paradigms with the historical experience of several theories being developed simultaneously. I shall consider Laudan's response to such issues in Chapter 5.

Is Kuhn's notion of the paradigm so seriously flawed? He recognises that his early treatment of the paradigm concept was 'badly confused' (Kuhn, 1970b, p. 234). Indeed, he has endeavoured to clarify the concept of the paradigm (Kuhn, 1977, ch. 12) and he now favours the use of the phrase 'disciplinary matrix' instead of 'paradigm'. This is because the concept is 'disciplinary' in the sense that it provides some common features that the practitioners within a particular discipline share and it is a 'matrix' because it is 'composed of ordered elements of various sorts, each requiring further specification'. The constituent elements of the paradigm are also dealt with in more detail. Kuhn focuses upon three of these: *symbolic generalisations, models* and *exemplars*. The first of these, symbolic generalisations, refers to aspects such as mathematical symbols which, when cast in logical form, are readily recognised and accepted by the group. Models provide the group with a useful means of analysing the phenomena that interests them; such models can be designed for a particular situation or reflect more generally a 'metaphysical commitment' to a certain perspective. Exemplars are solutions to problems that the group accepts and forms the basis for much of the work undertaken by them.

Johnson (1983) has sought to develop these notions further when considering economics. He is concerned to articulate a more robust conception of paradigms that may prove helpful to economists and recasts Kuhn's reformulation in the following manner. He identifies four features of paradigms that he considers to be readily applicable to economics: they are fundamental theoretical assumptions; methods of analysis and focal variables; basic issues; and professional relationships. Fundamental theoretical assumptions refer to Kuhn's 'symbolic generalisations'. In the context of economics this could refer to the classical economists' general acceptance of the wages fund doctrine and a subsistence theory of wages; also Keynesians tend to assume that the unfettered forces of the market do not guarantee full employment. Methods of analysis may refer to the relatively heavy use of econometric techniques, or conversely, axiomatic reasoning within the context of alternative paradigms. Focal variables would relate to distinctions between, for example, micro- and macroeconomic variables. Basic issues refer to aspects such as growth, employment and equity that form the 'puzzles' of particular groups.

Johnson believes that these characteristics of paradigms are relatively straightforward when applied to economics. However, he regards the question of professional relationships as problematic and in order to deal with this he introduces the notion of the 'purposive function' of a group. This refers to the goals and purposes to which the group's activities are geared. For example, the purposive function of the classical economists was to maximise the growth of the economy and once we recognise this much of their particular theories falls into place. The purposive function of the Keynesian paradigm is a concern with the attainment and maintenance of full employment.

Johnson believes that the purposive functions prove useful in distinguishing between intra-paradigm development (normal science) and inter-paradigm change (revolutions). In providing a group with a purpose it will exert a significant affect upon the other features of the paradigm such as methods and basic issues. Concerning inter-paradigm change it may give us stronger clues as to why a particular paradigm is experiencing difficulties and a revolution may be imminent. Take the Keynesian paradigm with its goal of maintaining full employment: since the late 1960s many economists have seen inflation increasingly as the aspect of the economy that deserves greater attention and the goal of groups such as the monetarists is often seen as being more directed towards the defeat of inflation. In so far as this has become a widespread view the emphasis upon maintaining full employment has weakened and with it the dominance of the Keynesian paradigm.

Concerning the notion of normal science, this has also met with much criticism. Popper (1970) has, not surprisingly, proved to be a consistent and vigorous critic of many aspects of Kuhn's work. He is particularly unhappy with what he perceives to be the uncritical and dogmatic nature of normal science, indeed he cites Kuhn's claim that the transition to normal science is marked by the abandonment of critical discourse. However, this highlights an important difference between Kuhn and Popper, which helps to explain the latter's unease. Popper attempts to prescribe what is, methodologically, good for us; Kuhn, on the other hand, is describing what he believes to be the actual development of scientific endeavour. Popper also dislikes the primacy given to 'puzzle-solving' within normal science as he suspects that this is indicative of such activity being largely unconcerned with tackling fundamental problems. The dominant paradigm is something that Popper also disagrees with – he believes that the coexistence of two or three paradigms is more usual. Indeed, he suggests that there is often 'constant and fruitful' discussion between adherents of competing paradigms. Watkins (1970) reiterates the general flavour of Popper's criticism of normal science; whilst acknowledging that a degree of dogmatism is not always undesirable he feels that normal science is too dogmatic. This is due to the fact that everyone working within a particular normal scientific framework is attempting to verify their paradigm-induced expectations. As a result no one endeavours to be critical, or sceptical, of the ruling paradigm.

Kuhn (1970b, p. 247) does not accept that normal science need necessarily become a dogmatic exercise. He believes that normal science permits more detailed and esoteric work which will lead to difficulties being discovered. Neither does he feel that normal science should be treated as a case of 'might being right'.

Despite Kuhn's views, some economists have viewed normal science as being potentially dogmatic and domineering. Benjamin Ward (1972) has employed the Kuhnian framework to consider whether orthodox, neo-classical economics can be regarded as a science. He argues that it does possess a number of the characteristics that are symptomatic of a normal scientific tradition. However, he raises several points as to whether this is desirable. For example, when considering puzzle-solving, he writes:

> The point is not so much to solve the problem, but to make an ingenious attempt at solution within the conventional framework of puzzles. There is thus some risk that economic science may degenerate into a series of self-contained methodological explorations which are not closely tied to that real world which is the normal subject of investigation. (Ward, 1972, p. 19)

This is precisely the type of argument raised in Chapter 1 by critics of the excessive use of mathematics, as mathematics is seen by many as an excuse to display one's virtuosity in mathematical manipulation. He also considers the notion of 'stylised facts' – false, or exaggerated, assumptions which are commonly accepted by economists when undertaking theoretical analysis. The axioms of indifference curve analysis would be a case in point. Ward believes that such assumptions can be easily used as a means of immunising theories from difficulties: 'To what extent are stylized facts used to conceal anomalies, to discourage consideration of topics that would be destructive of the framework of consensus of economic science?' (Ward, 1972, p. 22).

He also considers (pp. 28–31) how the normal scientific tradition within orthodox economics does serve as a potent control device. In this sense, Kuhn's concept of a 'disciplinary' matrix might have a sharper and more appropriate connotation than he imagined! This operates through the way that graduates and postgraduates are trained in economics: they are usually exposed to a strong diet of orthodox, neo-classical economics and this is supplemented by a thorough training in mathematical and econometric techniques. The structure of the profession is such that the leading practitioners, who serve as the example to follow for the majority of younger economists, largely adopt a conventional framework and formal techniques in their analyses and this helps to reinforce the hold of orthodoxy over the profession.

Ward also believes that the allocation of research funds acts as a means of maintaining a more conservative brand of economics in control. Governments and businesses are more likely to offer funds to 'safe' economists and institutions – by this I mean economists who are not too radical. This acquisition of research funds is an important part of the orthodox normal scientific tradition. With such funds they can attract what the group regard as the 'best' researchers and this will have spin-offs in the form of attracting better-quality postgraduate students to their institution.

Although orthodox economics resembles a Kuhnian normal scientific tradition, Ward argues that it is a group in crisis. He believes that there are a number of 'puzzles' that are increasingly becoming anomalous. Amongst these he cites the inability to satisfactorily integrate microeconomics with macroeconomics; the failure to incorporate theories of imperfect competition within a general equilibrium framework; the difficulties for conceptual analysis posed by externalities; and the increasing problems being faced with the application of econometrics.

These views are shared by other economists. For example, Canterbury and Burkhardt (1983) write:

> If we look at the dominant paradigm in economics, we see, in fact, that the discipline has not progressed very far, and, despite a certain avowal of positivist values, the protective belt (from refutation) functions there more like a chastity belt than even Kuhn and Lakatos would consider acceptable for a practising science. (p. 22)

Wiles (1983) believes that the orthodox paradigm is more of a bad habit than a good idea:

> Accepted paradigms stifle basic thought. They are only a social necessity, or a crutch, or – still worse – a shibboleth, and the society of scientists should be rearranged to do without them. This point is of vital importance when reform is being discussed. (p. 80)

What of revolutions within Kuhn's scheme? Popper (1970) and Lakatos (1970) have both expressed misgivings over what they see as the 'conversion' involved when revolutions occur. They liken this to an experience where a new perspective suddenly becomes fashionable and trendy and they both feel that revolutions are not entirely irrational leaps from one paradigm to another. Instead, some form of rational comparison between two alternative perspectives is usually possible. Watkins (1970) also raises several questions concerning revolutions: do paradigms enjoy a monopoly? Is there no interregnum between one paradigm falling and another replacing it? Are paradigm changes as sudden as in a '*Gestalt*-switch'? This latter refers to *Gestalt* psychology where those interesting drawings are viewed, such as the one where we see either a beautiful woman or an old hag, the implication being that a new paradigm encourages us to see things very differently, very suddenly. He believes that the answers to all these questions are negative and therefore Kuhn's explanation of revolutions is rendered unsatisfactory.

Kuhn (1970b) has rejected the above claims. He dismisses Popper's view of 'permanent revolutions' in science as being untenable. Instead, scientists need fully to explore and live within a particular scientific framework before it can be broken and he argues that the '*Gestalt*-switch' hypothesis is not an accurate depiction of his position on revolutions. He has always spoken of a transitional period between the rejection of one paradigm and the acceptance of another; indeed, we need to take each revolution on its own merits. This can only be done by undertaking a thorough historical analysis of the episode in question and such an analysis will need to consider carefully the structure of a group's commitment prior to and after a change in paradigm.

Kuhn has also sought to clarify that paradigms are not necessarily monolithic structures that dominate a whole field of scientific activity. Rather, different sciences will have fields of specialisation within which a particular paradigm may be dominant. In the context of economics it may, therefore, be possible that industrial, development or public sector economics each possess distinct paradigms and as a result it is possible to experience mini-revolutions within a particular area that can leave the mainstream of economics largely untouched.

Also, Kuhn does not accept that his account of revolutions necessarily implies irrational changes in allegiance from one paradigm to another. Although he continues to argue that different paradigms are unlikely to be directly comparable, there are criteria that can be employed to help form the basis of a rational choice. Kuhn (1977, ch. 13) identifies five features that are important for helping us to evaluate the adequacy of theories: they are accuracy; consistency; scope; simplicity; and fruitfulness. A theory which is accurate should be capable of deducing consequences which have some agreement with empirical reality. Consistency refers primarily to the internal logic of the theory. Breadth of scope should help to extend the applicability of the theory beyond the particular features that it was originally designed to deal with. Simplicity is where a theory helps to render phenomena orderly and explicable which otherwise would be confused, or even chaotic. Fruitfulness is where a new theory discerns relationships that were previously unrecognised which are important to the development of future research activity.

What do economists make of revolutionary science? Bronfenbrenner (1971) argues that in economics we cannot strictly apply the Kuhnian framework. As noted above he has expressed doubts about the notion of the paradigm which have implications for revolutions in economics. He believes that within economics the process of 'synthesis' allows old theories to survive rather than to be completely displaced. Also, he feels, along with Canterbury and Burkhardt and Wiles, that the adherence to normal science within economics is more tenacious. Indeed, Gordon (1965) and Baumberger (1977) argue that Kuhnian revolutions in economics do not occur.

Others believe that Kuhnian revolutions have occurred in economics. Let us consider the example of the Keynesian Revolution which, for example, Mehta (1977 and 1979) and Stanfield (1974) believe to be a good example of a Kuhnian revolution, so let us outline the process of this revolution. By the 1930s some features of orthodox macroeconomics were becoming increasingly anomalous. This related particularly to the simple version of Say's Law, whereby supply is said to create its own demand, thereby ruling out the serious possibility of market gluts and depression. This arises largely through the demand for money playing only a transactions role. Hoarding was not considered to be feasible, therefore money would find its way into circulation via investment and consumption. Furthermore, flexibility of prices, in both goods and labour, was generally assumed, therefore if short-term gluts did occur, the adjustment process towards equilibrium was assumed to be both relatively smooth and speedy. These views were something of a mixture of strands of classical economics and neo-classical economics. The purposive functions of these schools did not render unemployment a significant problem: for example, I have already noted how the distribution of factor shares, assuming full employment, was an important purposive function for classical economists. For neo-classical economists, one of their main goals, within their analytical system, was to consider the most efficient allocation of fully-employed resources.

Consequently, attention was not directed towards the level of unemployment in such frameworks. Indeed Keynes, when criticising A. C. Pigou, whom he considered to be a good representative of the orthodox view which he was attacking, accused him of making unrealistic assumptions (stylised facts) that assumed away the very problems that we were interested in. According to Keynes, Pigou assumed that there was full employment and a state of constant expectation.

This is suggestive of an anomalous crisis-ridden stage within macroeconomics and it certainly did appear to be the case. Around the turn of the century a period of extraordinary research was embarked upon where several economists were concentrating their efforts upon the anomalous area. As Stanfield (1974) points out, economists such as John A. Hobson, Ralph Hawtrey, Joseph Schumpeter and Wesley Clair Mitchell were articulating different explanations of cyclical depressions. In Sweden during the 1920s and 1930s several economists, including Gunnar Myrdal, Bertil Ohlin and David Davidson were anticipating much that was to appear in J. M. Keynes' *General Theory* in 1936. Michel Kalecki, a Polish economist, published work in the early 1930s which some believe to be more complete than the *General Theory*.

However, it was not until the publication of the *General Theory* that this extraordinary research previously undertaken began to take the shape of an alternative paradigm with prospects for the development of a normal scientific tradition and the analysis within this book provided the conceptual basis for some form of government counter-cyclical policy. It is difficult to imagine the shift in world view that this entailed. The so-called 'Treasury View' of that era frowned upon the budget being unbalanced. The budget was largely regarded as an exercise in bookkeeping where the government's annual expenditure and revenue were balanced. Also public works programmes for alleviating unemployment were often treated with suspicion; such schemes were liable to lead to what we now refer to as 'crowding-out'. This is where increases in public expenditure lead to reductions in private investment and consumption, thereby creating no extra, or little extra, employment. The *General Theory*, with its analysis of multiplier effects, did much to counter such arguments.

Furthermore, Keynes' work placed far more emphasis upon aggregate analysis, and the distinction of different demands for money (that is, transactions, precautionary and speculative) provided new insights. In short, there were a number of significant achievements that began to attract an enduring group of adherents. The Keynesian theory possessed simplicity; it provided an explanation for phenomena that were previously unintelligible, it had scope because it could be utilised and developed to study more than the level of employment (for example, growth economics); and it was fruitful because it could stimulate much research activity. Therefore, on Kuhn's criteria for adopting a new paradigm it would seem to score highly. Also, as Kuhn points out, the earliest and most enthusiastic recruits to a new paradigm come from the younger generation. This was certainly the case with Keynesianism. Young economists such as Joan Robinson, Richard Kahn and Roy Harrod were very committed. Keynes' position at Cambridge enabled him to teach such young talent and they played an important role in continuing, and articulating, the tradition bequeathed to them by Keynes after his death in 1946. Also more traditional economists such as Friedrich Hayek, A. C. Pigou and Dennis Robertson, who were less enthusiastic about Keynes' ideas' tended to 'fade away', as Kuhn predicted – they found themselves swimming against a tide that was too strong for them.

The setting for a revolutionary change-over to Keynes therefore seems to fit the Kuhnian scheme quite well, but did it lead to the development of a normal scientific tradition? The new paradigm, contained in the *General Theory*, was far from fully articulated. This meant that there were plenty of 'puzzles' to occupy researchers. Apart from conceptual 'puzzles' there were empirical ones also, indeed this was arguably the most explicit feature of Keynesian normal science. Empirical investigations of demand for money functions, consumption functions and multiplier magnitudes proliferated. This in itself did much to stimulate the development of econometric techniques within economics, also the academic journals became increasingly devoted to 'puzzles' surrounding the *General Theory*. In fact, Keynes was the editor of the *Economic Journal* when the book was published. In response to Pigou's criticisms that he was including articles in the journal largely devoted to his own ideas, Keynes defended himself by arguing that 'everyone' was discussing his ideas. Therefore it was legitimate for him to devote much space in the *Economic Journal* to articles related to his work.

The widespread adherence of Keynesianism, particularly in the UK during the 1950s and 1960s, led to textbooks being written that devoted large sections to macroeconomics. These presented Keynesian ideas in straightforward geometrical and algebraic forms, the 'Keynesian Cross' and *IS–LM* versions being most common. Consequently, widespread agreement over 'symbolic generalisations' was achieved and this is another important indication of a normal scientific tradition. There are a group of economists, known as Post-Keynesians, who would question whether Keynes' work was accurately interpreted after his death and I shall have something to say about this in my next chapter, but the consensus that existed has now broken down. In terms of macroeconomics we are very much in a Kuhnian crisis situation. We have assorted Keynesians, monetarists, rational expectationists, general equilibrium theorists, Austrians, Marxists and Institutionalists, to name only a few, competing to explain the stagflation of the late 1960s and 1970s. However, it would seem to be the case that there was a revolution and a subsequent period of normal science that showed strong similarities with the work of Kuhn.

Despite its limitations, Kuhn's methodological framework appears to offer more to economists than Popper. As previously noted, Kuhn is more concerned with methodological description, than with prescription and I feel that this presents us with a more realistic, and less Utopian, view of scientific practice. Although Kuhn's schema by no means exactly fits economics – no one methodology will achieve this – his structured elements have proved helpful to us and I believe that this applies particularly to the history of economic thought. Kuhn has influenced the way in which some of this work is undertaken and his guidelines have aided writers in producing more structured and comprehensive work (several of the articles cited above are evidence of this).

Also, Kuhn's work is an encouragement to those interested in the sociology of economic science – something which Popper has little time for. Little work has been done in this area, Ward (1972) and Eichner *et al.* (1983) being notable exceptions.

Even if we do not like all aspects of the path that Kuhn has beaten he has given us something to work with and this is precisely what the methodologists who form the subject of the next two chapters have attempted to pursue.

4 Lakatos and Economics

The limitations of the Popperian and Kuhnian methodologies have contributed toward economists increasingly turning to the work of Imre Lakatos (1922–74) for methodological succour. Lakatos' approach is interesting because, as we have seen above, he was critical of both Popper and Kuhn, and his methodology is something of a synthesis of aspects of these two approaches.

Before considering this it will prove instructive, as with Popper, to refer to some biographical details about Lakatos' life as they clearly affected his methodological outlook. He was born in Hungary where he eventually became an active member of the resistance movement against the Nazi occupation of that country. Being Jewish he changed his name twice, eventually opting for Lakatos ('locksmith'). His mother and grandmother perished in Auschwitz. After the war Lakatos, who was by then a Communist, became in 1947 an official in the Hungarian Ministry of Education. However, his independent way of thinking led him to be considered a 'revisionist' and this resulted in his spending three years, from 1950–53 in prison. During the Hungarian uprising of 1956 he was warned of his imminent re-arrest and this prompted him to flee to the West, initially to Cambridge, where he worked on his doctorate in mathematics, his original interest. In 1960 he moved to the London School of Economics, where he became a lecturer, and his interest in philosophy of science and methodology was re-awakened by the contact he had there with Popper (see Worrall, 1976, for other details of Lakatos' life).

Some of the traumatic events cited above, not surprisingly, affected his methodological views. For example, he was more vociferous than Popper in wishing to develop a demarcation criterion between science and pseudo-science. For Lakatos this was a question 'of vital social and political relevance' which had 'grave ethical and political implications'. Also, there is a clear commitment to a more tolerant and liberal attitude towards methodology and both of these features may well be a reaction to some of his bitter and tragic experiences. It will become clear how these two aspects of his methodology appear to be incompatible and create tensions within his approach.

The other main stimulants to his interest in methodology were the limitations he saw in other methodologies. He rejected inductivism, and even attempts to derive an inductive probability calculus, along similar lines to those considered by Popper. However, despite his broad sympathies with Popper, he was unhappy with certain aspects of falsificationism. For example, he recognised the implications of the Duhem–Quine Thesis for testability – we have seen the implication that this held for the form of falsificationism that we considered in Chapter 2. This is what Lakatos termed 'naïve' falsificationism, where an attempt is made to falsify a single theory or hypothesis. Lakatos argued that this is invalid on two counts. Firstly, we are more likely to be testing a *series of theories*. Here the test of one hypothesis entails auxiliary hypotheses as well as certain initial conditions and consequently any test of a theory is as much an indirect test of a series of interconnected theories. A naïve falsificationist is interested in *eliminating* a single hypothesis; a sophisicated falsificationist, such as Lakatos, is concerned with groups of theories and the circumstances under which it is reasonable to *save* them. Secondly, Lakatos felt that some of Popper's rules for empirical science were far too severe: this applied particularly to the treatment of new theories, which Lakatos felt often deserved careful nurturing. This point also led Lakatos to disagree with Popper's quest for 'instant' rationality whereby we eliminate theories and hope, in the process, that we have moved closer to the truth. Lakatos believed that the attainment of rationality worked more slowly. Indeed we shall see how rational judgements concerning theories are made largely in retrospect.

Another point on which Lakatos disagreed with Popper was that he felt that verification, but not the 'trivial' ones associated with inductivism, could, and often did, play a useful role in the development of theories.

Lakatos accused Kuhn of many things, especially of encouraging 'irrationalism' and this was particularly the case during revolutionary episodes. We saw in the last chapter how some element of 'religious conversion' and acts of faith usually played some part in the transition from one paradigm to another. Also, Kuhn argued that it was difficult to compare and contrast different paradigms, thereby rendering rational comparison between them problematic. Lakatos felt unhappy with this and his methodology sought to provide some means for rational comparisons between different paradigms.

Lakatos also disliked the Kuhnian notions of the dominant paradigm and normal science, believing them to be unhealthy. He disliked methodological monopolies, believing them to be breeding grounds for dogmatism, and favoured competition between paradigms. This last feature became an important element in his approach. Furthermore, he did not accept the Kuhnian view of dominant paradigms as being historically accurate. Rather, he envisaged two or more perspectives rivalling one another. Indeed, Lakatos saw science as being conducted very much in terms of a three-cornered fight between, at least, two rival paradigms and nature.

How did Lakatos respond to these limitations? His approach is an attempt to appraise how well, or otherwise, a group of theories have performed. This also relates to Lakatos' demarcation criterion.

THE METHODOLOGY OF SCIENTIFIC RESEARCH PROGRAMMES

To accomplish this, and to deal with the limitations of Popper and Kuhn, Lakatos developed his methodology of scientific research programmes (MSRP). A research programme consists of two main elements, the hard core with its protective belt, and the positive heuristic. The hard core is described in the following terms:

> All scientific research programmes may be characterised by their 'hard core'. The negative heuristic of the programme forbids it to direct the *modus tollens* [attempts at refutation] at this hard core. Instead, we must use our ingenuity to articulate or even invent 'auxiliary hypotheses', which form a protective belt around this core, and we must redirect the *modus tollens* to these. It is this protective belt of auxiliary hypotheses which has to bear the brunt of tests and get adjusted and re-adjusted, or even completely replaced to defend the thus hardened core. (Lakatos, 1978, p. 48)

Consequently, the hard core consists of a set of basic axioms and hypotheses which the proponents of a particular research programme accept without question.

The positive heuristic performs a less defensive function than that of the hard core – it refers to the set of puzzles, problems and theories that deal with anomalies and help to drive the entire research programme forward and is characterised in the following terms:

> Few theoretical scientists engaged in research programmes pay undue attention to 'refutations'. They have a long-term research policy which anticipates these refutations. This research policy, or order of research, is set out – in more or less detail – in the *positive heuristic* of the research programme. The negative heuristic specifies the 'hard core' of the programme which is 'irrefutable' by the

methodological decision of its proponents; the positive heuristic consists of a partially articulated set of suggestions or hints on how to change, develop the 'refutable variants', of the research programme, how to modify, sophisticate, the 'refutable' protective belt. (Lakatos, 1978, p. 50).

There are clear analogies here with Kuhn. The hard core is reminiscent of the paradigm and the positive heuristic of normal science and such analogies were actually accepted by both Kuhn and Lakatos. However, there are differences. For example, Lakatos regarded the hard core as being fixed, whereas Kuhn argued that the paradigm normally required further articulation. Also Lakatos' construction operates very differently from that of Kuhn. Lakatos emphasised the relative performances of rival theories and it is through such comparisons that we can begin to demarcate science from pseudo-science, and also to determine whether a revolutionary transition, from one research programme to another, has occurred. On the question of demarcation, Lakatos felt that his approach aided us when distinguishing between 'progressive' (scientific) and 'degenerating' (pseudo-scientific) research programmes. A 'progressive' research programme is one that possesses excess content, either theoretical or empirical, over its rival, some of which is corroborated (see Lakatos, 1978, p. 34). In contrast to this we may encounter degenerating programmes that are:

> . . . fabricated only in order to accommodate known facts. Has, for instance, Marxism ever predicted a stunning novel fact successfully? Never! It has some famous unsuccessful predictions. It predicted the absolute impoverishment of the working class. It predicted that the first socialist revolution would take place in the industrially most developed society. It predicted that socialist societies would be free of revolutions . . . Thus the early predictions of Marxism were bold and stunning, but they failed . . . But their auxiliary hypotheses were all cooked up after the event to protect Marxian theory from the facts'. (Lakatos, 1978, pp. 5–6)

Lakatos' notions of 'progressive' and 'degenerating' research programmes are important; I have already referred to the significance he attached to the demarcation of science from pseudo-science. They also form the basis for explaining revolutionary changes where scientists switch their allegiance from one research programme to another. Once a programme is degenerating there is the prospect, ultimately, that it may be 'eliminated' or 'falsified'. Falsification does not necessarily mean that a particular perspective has been empirically rejected – falsification, for Lakatos, can only arise within the context of the arrival of a new research programme to challenge an existing one and the new arrival has to offer some excess and novel content *vis-à-vis* its predecessor. If in turn some of this excess content is corroborated then the possibility of eliminating or falsifying the old, existing programme becomes real. Indeed a falsification in this sense refers more to an older programme being shelved and people switching to a more progressive new arrival.

Lakatos, being a liberal methodologically, qualifies the way in which such elimination and rejection of research programmes can be achieved. For example, he argues that a budding research programme should be treated leniently. If a new programme displays promise and is progressive, but not yet fully capable of dealing with aspects that an existing programme can deal with, 'it should be sheltered for a while from a more powerful established rival' (Lakatos, 1978, p. 71). Such new programmes may only begin their lives by explaining old facts in a 'novel' way – this would be grounds for seriously entertaining the new programme and enabling it to develop the potential it appears to hold. This developmental period, for budding research programmes, can be quite substantial. For example, Lakatos argues that it can take 'decades' for a new programme to become theoretically progressive. This period can be extended further before the theory can provide propositions amenable to empirical testing.

Consequently, the process of eliminating a degenerating programme by a progressive new rival, can be a protracted affair. Lakatos also argues, therefore, that 'crucial experiments' are rarely ever seen as such when conducted; they are usually only seen as such when viewed retrospectively.

The process of elimination is made more difficult by Lakatos' liberal attitude towards certain degenerating programmes. As he notes, once a programme enters a degenerating phase it 'occasionally happens' that 'a little revolution or a creative shift in its positive heuristic may push it forward again'. Indeed, Lakatos made this point more forcefully when he wrote:

One *must* realise that one's opponent even if lagging badly behind may still stage a comeback. No advantage for one side can ever be regarded as absolutely conclusive. There is never anything inevitable about its defeat. Thus pigheadedness, like modesty, has more 'rational' scope. *The scores of the rival sides, however, must be recorded and publicly displayed at all times.* (Lakatos, 1978, p. 113, italics as in the original)

However, elsewhere he suggests (Lakatos, 1978, p. 69) that we should not necessarily stick to a degenerating programme until 'all of its heuristic power is exhausted'. The questions are, when do we know that its heuristic power is close to exhaustion, and can we not, by an act of imagination rejuvenate it?

The flexibility implied in Lakatos' approach has led to the charge, notably from Feyerabend (1978), that 'anything goes': that is, it is almost reasonable, and rational, to adhere to almost any perspective one wishes. Lakatos (1978, p. 114) denies this. He argues that it may be rational to stay with a degenerating programme 'until it is overtaken by a rival *and even after*', but that its poor public performance should not be denied. Lakatos argued that this is not as licentious as it appears, for when a group stay with a degenerating programme, they should do so in private and editors of journals should not publish their papers nor research foundations grant them funds (Lakatos, 1978, p. 117).

CRITICISMS OF LAKATOS' APPROACH

This rather stern advice leads to clear tensions within Lakatos' system: on the one hand he is seeking to employ his demarcation criterion sharply, and on the other, his more liberal attitude towards falsification renders this task difficult, if not impossible. This is understandable. He was eager to ensure that new programmes, if promising, were given every chance to thrive. He did not want to see any established programme achieve a monopoly or the status of 'a Weltanschaung, or a sort of *scientific rigor*, setting itself up as an arbiter between explanation and non-explanation'. Therefore, if new and rival programmes are permitted to compete with such established programmes there is less chance that they will become complacent monopolies.

There are other difficulties that are associated with Lakatos' approach. Firstly, there is the general problem of a lack of definitions of key concepts and the rather unsystematic way in which Lakatos presented his ideas compounds this difficulty. For example, when considering the notion of the hard core I deliberately referred to it as a description, rather than a definition. In Lakatos' writings we do not receive any clear indication as to what should constitute the basic features of any hard core – this is important because it is the hard core which characterises any research programme. Ambiguities over what should form the hard core are likely to lead to the sort of difficulties posed by Kuhn's loose definition of a paradigm. We shall shortly see that this has certainly posed problems for economic applications of Lakatos' method. Also, Musgrave (1976, pp. 458–9) disputes Lakatos' treatment of the hard core as being fixed, once established, and 'irrefutable by fiat'. Musgrave argues the scientists frequently adjust and articulate their hard cores, also the history of science indicates that certain 'sacred' propositions are often changed in response to difficulties. We are also likely to encounter difficulties in distinguishing between propositions that fall in the hard core or the protective belt. The distinction is crucial because a protective belt proposition can, in principle, be subject to refutation, whereas a hard core proposition cannot. This could, and has, led to confusion, between economists as to what they can legitimately attempt to falsify or not, using Lakatos' approach.

Secondly, there are aspects relating to the positive heuristic that give cause for concern. It is highly questionable that scientists anticipate refutations and anomalies and devise long-term research strategies to cope with them. Newton-Smith (1981, pp. 84–5) points out that scientists typically respond to empirical and conceptual anomalies once they have arisen. He believes that the Lakatosian system does not provide us with the kind of early warning system that could anticipate anomalies. Furthermore, it is a waste of intellectual effort and resources to spend time anticipating anomalies. Interestingly, Lakatos recognised some of these points. In one of his historical case studies he noted 'not all developments in the programme were foreseen and planned when the positive heuristic was first sketched' (Lakatos, 1978, p. 67).

Musgrave raises another point regarding the positive heuristic, one that I referred to above. This concerns the question of when do we regard the positive heuristic as having proved incapable of dealing with anomalies? Could it not be more a case of the proponents within a particular programme lacking sufficient imagination and resourcefulness in devising ways of tackling such anomalies?

Musgrave was also critical of Lakatos' tendency, also noted above, to offer quite firm advice to editors of journals and research institutes on how they should treat degenerating programmes. Conversely, Lakatos later insisted that his methodology could provide no such guidance. Musgrave recognised that Lakatos' appraisal of competing programmes provides no *logical* basis for preferring one over another. But surely it is intended to provide us with some grounds for such a preference? If it is not then what is such an appraisal designed to achieve? Many of these criticisms are also forcefully reiterated in Laudan (1977, p. 77–8).

LAKATOS AND ECONOMICS

During the last few years economists have increasingly been looking to Lakatos' methodology. A notable landmark in this development was the publication of *Method and Appraisal in Economics*, edited by S. J. Latsis in 1976. This was a collection of essays specifically designed to assess how well Lakatos' approach could be applied to economics. The book has received very mixed reviews. For example, Agassi (1979), in a very dismissive review, felt that the authors had generally failed to appreciate the Popperian inheritance of Lakatos. Fulton (1984), in a constructive contribution to the discussion, feels that some of the contributions, and their applications, encountered difficulties that may have misdirected subsequent applications of the methodology of scientific research programmes within economies.

He recognised that many difficulties had been encountered in distinguishing between the concepts of hard cores, protective belts and positive heuristics.

Applications of neo-classical economics from the Latsis volume highlight some of the differences encountered.

Latsis (1976, p. 22) defines the hard core of neo-classical economics as constituting the following four propositions:

(1) Decision-makers have correct knowledge of the relevant features of their economic situation.
(2) Decision-makers *prefer* the best available alternative given their knowledge of the situation and of the means at their disposal.
(3) Given (1) and (2) situations generate their internal 'logic' and decision-makers *act appropriately to the logic of their situation*.
(4) Economic units and structures display stable, co-ordinated behaviour.

Blaug (1976, p. 161) defines the neoclassical programme in the following terms:

It is made up, first of all, of the principle of constrained maximization, 'Smith's postulate of the maximizing individual in a relatively free market', or what Friedman calls for short the 'maximization-of-returns hypothesis'. The principle of maximizing behaviour subject to constraints is then joined to the notion of general equilibrium in self-regulating competitive markets to produce the method of comparative statics, which is the economist's principal device for generating qualitative predictions of the signs rather than the magnitudes of its critical variables. The 'hard core' or metaphysical part of this programme consists of weak versions of competitive theory, namely rational economic calculations, constant tastes, independence of decision-making, perfect knowledge, perfect certainty, perfect mobility of factors, et cetera.

In his review of the Latsis volume, Archibald (1979, p. 309) considered the neo-classical hard core as being 'that economic agents are to be modelled as rational people "making the best of a bad job", which usually means choosing, or maximising under constraint'. He also pointed out that the definition of any economic research programme needed to be clear but he had doubts as to whether this had been achieved. Fulton (1984) and Remenyi (1979) provide slightly different and more detailed definitions. Although there are clear similarities between these three hard cores it is the differences in detail which can create difficulties. How serious a problem is this for the application of Lakatos to economics?

Fulton recognises the seriousness of this problem. He argues that it is the applications, not the methodology, that have been at fault. He believes that although a number of common threads between the hard cores are discernable they are generally imprecisely stated. Furthermore, the adoption of 'neo-classical' economics requires a much clearer delineation. This covers a very wide area of economic theory. Fulton makes the point, following Lakatos, that the series of theories constituting a research programme should be some distinct part of a whole discipline. Therefore, rather than seeking to view the whole area of neo-classical economics we would be better advised to concentrate on one aspect of it, for example, capital theory .

Fulton believes that an extra element of the Lakatosian framework should be added, that of presuppositions – these are statements that are imprecise and such statements are made prior to outlining the hard core. He feels that this would be a helpful exercise as basic presuppositions often tend to be particularly contentious, also the detailing of such 'metaphysical elements' can often prove helpful as conceptual disputes between alternative research programmes are frequently of a philosophical nature.

In developing this modification of Lakatos' approach, Fulton focuses on the concept of the neo-classical production function, which consists of theories of production, distribution, growth and technical change. His presuppositions are:

(1) The central economic problem is that of allocating scarce resources among alternative uses.
(2) Economic theories are abstract, general theories based on deductive models.
(3) Economic theory is based on individual entities, for example, consumers and firms.
(4) These individual entities have full knowledge of the relevant circumstances of their economic situation.
(5) Each individual acts rationally.
(6) Each individaul is a maximising agent.
(7) Economic theory is essentially concerned with comparative static equilibrium.
(8) Economic theory is within the tradition of positive science.
(9) As well as verbal exposition, theories should, if possible, be presented in as rigorous mathematical form as possible.

Fulton's hard core is based on three features which we assume for each firm – the existence of a production function; the principle of diminishing returns; and that factor inputs are continuously substitutable. From this the positive heuristic of the programme will offer the following directives:

(1) Construct models based on profit-maximisation or cost-minimisation.
(2) Specify the market conditions for firms, consumers and inputs that ensure that a determinate equilibrium is achieved. Here the use of the assumption of perfectly competitive markets is important.
(3) Models should be constructed at an aggregate level on an analogous basis with the micro- or individual-level models.
(4) Refine our theories by introducing more realistic complications such as imperfect markets.

Fulton's analysis does not attempt to make bold assertions about degeneracy or progressiveness. Instead, he makes more modest claims for Lakatos' approach:

> The MSRP employed in the proper context and in the proper way will provide a more than useful method of historical appraisal, but it will not provide a simple panacea which will give definite answers to comparisons between various schools of economic thought, as some

of its early exponents in economics had apparently hoped. Nevertheless it can further our understanding of both past and present-day economics by presenting a means of clarifying economic theories, by highlighing the many elements, particularly the implicit metaphysical elements, in these theories, and by providing an impartial, but of course criticisable, standard for judging these theories. Thus the MSRP presents itself as a valuable tool to anyone seeking to understand the history or present state of economics. (Fulton, 1984, p. 204)

Given the difficulties encountered with Lakatos' approach, this more modest assessment of its usefulness for economists seems appropriate.

In another interesting application of Lakatos' methodology to economics Cross (1982) endeavours to consider the recent development of monetarism. He begins his consideration by referring to some of the difficulties of applying Lakatos' method to economics. For example, how do we distinguish between a proposition that forms part of the hard core or its protective belt? As noted above, such a distinction can be an extremely fine one to make. He refers to the proposition 'unemployment is independent of aggregate demand in the long-run, in the absence of government intervention' as being a possible candidate for a hard core monetarist proposition. However, he feels it could equally form a protective belt hypothesis which, subject to empirical testing, could prove to be dispensable. Indeed Cross argues that 'views as to which propositions are more fundamental have not been widely accepted or time-invariate enough for us to be able to draw a clear distinction between hard core and protective belt propositions in economics' (p. 331). He abandons the distinction between hard core and protective belt, arguing that a helpful way to proceed is to distinguish between *ex ante* and *ex post* hard core propositions. The former are those propositions which are regarded as being open to challenge, and the latter refers to those propositions which, over time, the programme has seen fit to hold on to despite logical and empirical criticism.

Cross then proceeds to consider the historical development of monetarism. He identifies a monetarist positive heuristic directive as 'explain sustained variations in the rate of inflation by sustained prior variations in the rate of monetary expansion'. However, we would need to include other 'co-determinants' within the monetarist scheme such as interest rates, output, employment and foreign exchange rates.

Cross' sketch suggests that between 1956, when Friedman restated the Quantity Theory of Money, and 1973, monetarism was progressive

Important developments included the natural-rate of unemployment and the related notion of the expectations-augmented Phillips Curve as well as the monetary theory of the balance of payments which took into account the significance of exchange rates. These two theoretically progressive notions received some empirical confirmation as they predicted the increase in unemployment, with strong inflation, and the simultaneously increasing international inflation rates of the late 1960s.

However, Cross believes that since 1973, monetarism has exhibited signs of degeneracy. There has been contradictory evidence, such as the holdings of money balances being far higher in the UK and US than are consistent with a stable demand for money function, also the dramatic increase in unemployment in the UK since 1978 is not easily explained by the natural rate of unemployment. Cross (1984, p. 95) argues that the monetarist reaction to this adverse evidence has been to resort to *ad hoc* defences. He gives several examples, 'mismanagement of monetary policy', 'structural change in the monetary system', 'confidence factors', 'supply factors' and 'the world recession'.

Cross provides us with an interesting application of Lakatos' method. However, he recognises that it has its limitations. For example, there is a sense in which it is not a purely Lakatosian treatment of the development of monetarism. This is due to there being no comparison of rival programmes, especially the Keynesian, also Cross admits that his retrospective analysis cannot furnish us with a reliable guide as to what his story, told in the year 2000, would be.

Other writers have sought to consider certain episodes in the history of economic thought using Lakatos' framework. The first application was that of Blaug (1976) in which he paid particular attention to the Keynesian revolution. He is strongly critical of Kuhn's approach and favours Lakatos' attempts to de-emphasise sociological factors when considering the history of science. Indeed, Lakatos regarded historical analyses that relied heavily upon sociological factors as a means of disguising their conceptual 'illiteracy'. It is the ideas that are important. With such considerations in mind he sought to distinguish between 'internal' and 'external' factors when considering historical development. 'Internal' factors emphasise the problem-situation facing a programme at that time and the internal consistency, and logic, of the theories designed to resolve it. Lakatos wanted 'internal' factors to be the primary means whereby we could rationally consider how a particular programme had developed. Political, psychological or sociological factors are typically considered 'external'. Although Lakatos wanted 'internal' factors to dominate in historical analyses he did recognise that 'external' factors would often provide supplementary detail that needed to be considered.

Blaug argues that Keynes' hard core was essentially the same as that of the neo-classical research programme in so far as he employed concepts such as general equilibrium, perfect competition and comparative statics. He did depart from this hard core in two important respects: he did not regard the labour market as being perfect (his rejection of Say's Law therefore rendered the possibility of unemployment within his analysis); also he worked in aggregates rather than using the individualistic concepts of much orthodoxy.

Blaug sees the multiplier, consumption function and speculative demand for money as being protective belt concepts. The positive heuristic gave directives that enabled researchers to deal with empirical problems of the consumption function and further develop national income accounts. He feels that the Keynesian programme predicted novel features such as periods of sustained unemployment. He sees the Keynesian programme very much in terms of a progressive programme, replacing a degenerating programme because it possessed excess empirical content.

The reader may be wondering whether a similar story has not already been told in the previous chapter, employing the Kuhnian framework. There is a sense in which a Lakatosian framework may be a more realistic depiction of the Keynesian revolution. For example, Blaug is right to emphasise the neo-classical underpinnings of Keynes' work. However, Keynesianism has been seen as providing an alternative to neo-classical economics. This has led to much confusion and dispute as to the revolutionary nature of Keynes' work. Lakatos recognised some of the problems faced here:

> Indeed, *some of the most important research programmes in the history of science were grafted on to older programmes with which they were blatantly inconsistent* ... As the young grafted programme strengthens, the peaceful co-existence comes to an end, the symbiosis becomes competitive and the champions of the new programme try to replace the old programme altogether. (Lakatos, 1978, pp. 56–7, italics as in the original)

This might not be an inappropriate way to describe the development of Keynesianism. The *General Theory* was grafted on to the neo-classical system. Therefore in a conceptual sense it was never completely revolutionary, although some of the policy implications drawn from it were. However, others have argued (for example, Davidson, 1978; and

Shackle, 1974) that Keynes did intend a more radical departure from orthodoxy than is generally believed to have been the case. They argue that the *IS–LM* or 'neo-classical synthesis' versions of the *General Theory* are nothing less than a complete travesty of Keynes' intentions. Keynes seemingly placed great emphasis upon aspects such as expectations and uncertainty that appears to contradict the standard comparative static equilibrium approach contained in *IS–LM* analysis. In this case, within Lakatos' framework, it may be a case of the young programme actually losing the battle and being safely absorbed by the older programme. Many would regard this as an accurate portrayal of the Keynesian 'revolution'.

However, the Kuhnian analysis in Chapter 3 is more precise in dealing with features of the *General Theory*, especially when we take into account some of Kuhn's attempts to clarify paradigm characteristics. A sensible way to view a Kuhnian or Lakatosian analysis of the Keynesian revolution is that if used with subtlety and imagination they can both provide useful insights into that particular period of economic thought.

More generally, other writers have not shared the enthusiasm for applying Lakatos' approach to economics. Leijonhufvud (1976) and Hutchison (1976) see the differences between economics and physics as being so significant as to make the translation of Lakatos' methodology to economics highly problematic. Indeed, Hutchison makes much of the 'anything goes' criticisms of Lakatos that I considered above. In conclusion, Fulton's judicious summary seems to be the most appropriate way in which to view Lakatos' approach when applied to economics. Its very flexibility creates problems of definition as witnessed in the different hard cores of neo-classical economics considered above. Consequently, some of the more ambitious attempts to employ Lakatos' method for purposes of demarcation are doomed to disappointment and it seems to be most helpful when confined to analysing certain episodes in the history of economic thought.

5 Laudan and the Problems of Progress

In the last two chapters Larry Laudan was mentioned in the context of criticism of Kuhn and Lakatos. In response to such criticism, Laudan has developed his own methodology which essentially seeks to synthesise the best features of Kuhn and Lakatos with his own distinctive contribution. Laudan has been virtually ignored by economists and I find this surprising for two reasons: firstly, economists have paid much attention to Kuhn and Lakatos, therefore it would seem only natural that someone who seeks to take their approaches a step further should be the object of some interest to economists; secondly, it does appear, as we shall see below, that Laudan does have something to offer economists.

In this chapter I shall outline the essential features of Laudan's position, some of the criticisms that have been made of it and how helpful it could prove to economists.

SCIENCE AS PROBLEM-SOLVER

Laudan's methodology has been primarily articulated in his book *Progress and its Problems*, published in 1977. He argues that his approach, with suitable modifications, is applicable to 'all intellectual disciplines' and it is clear from this, as well as from numerous comments made in his book, that Laudan regards the social sciences, and therefore economics, as legitimate areas for the application of his methodology. Therefore, he clearly differs from Kuhn and Lakatos who were less enthusiastic about the social sciences endeavouring to employ their methodologies. However, Laudan never elaborates as to what is involved in a 'suitable modification' when applying his method to the social sciences.

Laudan argues that the central feature of science is problem-solving. Problems are the focal point, and the questions, of science whilst theories are designed to serve as the answers to such questions: 'The function of a theory is to resolve ambiguity, to reduce irregularity to uniformity, to show that what happens is somehow intelligible and predictable; it is this complex of functions to which I refer when I speak of theories as solutions to problems' (Laudan, 1977, p. 13).

Laudan then sets out to explain the different notions of problems and, most crucially for him, the ways in which we can assess the effectiveness of their solutions. He begins by making an important distinction between empirical and conceptual problems.

EMPIRICAL PROBLEMS

An empirical problem is something that is unusual in the real world under investigation. However, something will not be considered unusual or odd unless we take account of the 'context of inquiry' in which the problem arises. Theoretical frameworks, or paradigms, lay down clear indications as to what we should expect from our theories of the economy in different circumstances. Therefore, the standard 45° diagonal graph presentation of Keynes' theory would lead us to expect that an increase in government expenditure will lead to an increase in national income and employment. If, instead, it resulted in an increase in unemployment quite a few Keynesian eyebrows would be raised! I am assuming that there are no other serious deficiencies in the other components of aggregate demand. Under such circumstances the resulting increase in unemployment would, in the first instance, constitute an empirical problem for Keynesians.

Furthermore, Laudan argues that once we view empirical problems within their context of inquiry, it is frequently the case that an empirical problem for one paradigm is nothing of the sort for an alternative paradigm. The example just cited would be something that monetarists would actually expect – for them increased government expenditure leads to increased unemployment for the following reasons. Firstly, they believe that any increase in government expenditure tends to 'crowd out' private investment and consumption. However, this is likely to be a more serious phenomenon during periods of full employment. Increased government expenditure will often be financed by the government borrowing more money and this can easily lead to pressures within the money markets that will result in an increase in interest rates. Investment plans that are interest-elastic may well be seriously affected by such increases in interest rates. Alternatively, increases in government expenditure may be financed by increased taxation. Also, many monetarists believe that higher taxation leads to disincentive effects: that is, entrepreneurs and workers will not be prepared to maximise their respective efforts and this would result in both lower output and ultimately fewer jobs.

Also monetarists see increased government expenditure as likely to lead to an increase in the money supply if financed by the central bank. This being the case, inflation will result, under the monetarist scheme of things. Consequently, inflationary pressures will increase uncertainty, lead to misallocation of resources and further losses in jobs. For monetarists an increase in public expenditure, if resulting in increased unemployment, would be empirically expected.

Laudan categorises empirical problems in three ways: firstly, there are unsolved problems – these are problems that have resisted adequate solution by any theory; secondly, there are solved problems; and finally, we have anomalous problems which are unsolved by one theory, but solved by a competitor.

Laudan argues that we can identify scientific progress as occurring when either unsolved or anomalous empirical problems have found a solution. The status of unsolved problems is an important stimulant to progress in science. However, problems will only be 'potential' ones until one theory finds a solution for them. It is then that rival theories have a problem on their hands.

The empirical problem of the trade cycle springs to mind. Say's Law does not permit prolonged periods of depression and unemployment. The fact that sustained periods of depression were increasingly occurring during the nineteenth century, although casting doubt on Say's Law, would not count as an empirical problem against the classical economists until a rival theory had come up with a solution. We saw, in Chapter 3, how the efforts of William Stanley Jevons, J. A. Hobson and others were not regarded as satisfactory solutions to this empirical problem. However, the publication of Keynes' *General Theory* changed things. Here was a work that was widely regarded as providing a convincing explanation of the fact that a capitalist economy could experience sustained periods of unemployment. It was only then that the classical orthodoxy could be said to have been faced with a 'core anomaly'.

This is an interesting point. Laudan recognises that we are unlikely to know in advance the empirical problems that will pose serious threats to a theory. To begin with, the difficulties of measurement, testing, and so on, mean that we should not exaggerate, at least initially, the importance of an empirical problem. It could be more a problem of observation and the quirks of statistics. Also we need to realise that paradigms are typically a complex of solved and unsolved problems. Therefore, considering any empirical problem in isolation may not be a very good reflection of the general health of a paradigm. However, where competing theories have solved the empirical problem it does become more serious to the paradigm that cannot deal with it, as in the case of the classical school and trade cycles. This is important for Laudan because he emphasises the comparative nature of theory evaluation. He is unhappy with crudely empiricist approaches that seek to compare theories only against 'the facts'. These can prove to be misleading, and misguided, endeavours to gauge the effectiveness of theories against some 'objective' standard. A point that Laudan repeatedly emphasises is that the nature of a problem, and an acceptable solution to it, are frequently changing, that is, what is acceptable during one period will not be considered so later. Laudan believes that an empirical problem has been solved when scientists 'believe they understand why the situation propounded by the problem is the way it is' (Laudan, 1977, p. 22). He takes this a stage further by challenging the widely accepted view that problem solution necessarily implies the discovery of the truth:

> By way of contrast, I shall claim that: a theory may solve a problem so long as it entails even an *approximate* statement of the problem; in determining if a theory solves a problem, *it is irrelevant whether the theory is true or false, well or poorly confirmed,* what counts as a solution to a problem at one time will not necessarily be regarded as such at all times. (Laudan, 1977, p. 22, italics as in the original)

This is a very controversial position, something that we encounter in the next chapter in connection with Milton Friedman, and which Laudan, as we shall see, has been strongly criticised for holding. However, he is quite unrepentant about this. He argues that it is all very well Popper and Lakatos virtuously attempting to seek 'the truth', but the problem with this view is that such methodologists beg the question as to how we achieve this laudable objective. He feels that too much time is wasted in debating such intractable issues and his approach is therefore very much in the tradition of pragmatism.

For Laudan, the solution to an empirical problem is not something that requires an exact prediction from an experimental situation. Instead, empirical problems frequently find a solution via a more approximate correspondence between experiments and theories; indeed, such solutions are typically 'highly relative and comparative'.

CONCEPTUAL PROBLEMS

Laudan also pays much attention to the notion of conceptual problems. He feels that this issue has been virtually ignored by Kuhn and Lakatos. Indeed, he regards the emphasis placed upon the solution of empirical problems as a reflection of a rather naïve empiricist bias in our methodological attitudes and he regards conceptual problems as being at least as important as empirical ones. Conceptual problems can only arise within the context of a particular theory: they cannot exist independently of the theory that gave rise to them. A conceptual problem, for any theory (T) arises in two forms:

1. When T exhibits certain internal inconsistencies, or when its basic categories of analysis are vague and unclear, there are *internal conceptual problems*.

2. When T is in conflict with another theory or doctrine T¹, which proponents of T¹ believe to be rationally well founded, there are *external conceptual problems*. (Laudan, 1977, pp. 48–9, italics as in the original)

An interesting facet of conceptual problems is that of the methodologies associated with different theories. Laudan argues that the methodologies associated with particular theories *do* matter, sometimes decisively. The methodological well-foundedness of a theory can form one of the most important aspects of our conceptual appraisal of a theory, rather than being tangential to it:

> It is for precisely that reason that perceived methodological weaknesses have constituted serious, and often acute conceptual problems for any theory exhibiting them. It is for the same reason that the elimination of incompatibilities between a theory and the relevant methodology constitutes one of the most impressive ways in which a theory can improve its cognitive standing. (Laudan, 1977, p. 59)

Laudan believes that conceptual anomalies are frequently more serious than those posed by empirical problems. He realises how Duhem–Quine-type considerations, which cast doubt upon the conclusiveness of any particular empirical test, enable scientists to disregard unfavourable empirical results. Also, as noted above, this may be a sensible move given Laudan's doubts about placing too much emphasis upon empirical results, especially in view of their unreliability.

A conceptual problem, however, is not so easily dismissed. The seriousness of a conceptual problem is dependent, to some extent, upon its age and a problem that has only recently arisen may not be considered too serious, because scientists feel confident that they can deal with it. Once the problem proves resistant to such efforts it becomes increasingly serious.

Bringing together the notions of empirical and conceptual problems,

Laudan begins to formulate his more general view as to how we can assess the problem-solving effectiveness of any theory. The central feature of this appraisal is that solved problems, whether empirical or conceptual, form the key to scientific progress. From this we can arrive at the aim of science. For Laudan this is to '*maximize the scope of solved problems, while minimising the scope of anomalies and conceptual problems*' (Laudan, 1977, p. 66, italics as in the original).

RESEARCH TRADITIONS

It is at this stage that Laudan introduces his notion of the research tradition, which is analogous to Kuhn's paradigm and Lakatos' research programme. A research tradition is described in the following terms as a set of:

1. ... specific theories which exemplify and partially constitute it, some of these theories will be contemporaneous, others will be temporal successors of earlier ones;
2. Every research tradition exhibits certain *metaphysical* and *methodological* commitments which, as an ensemble, individuate the research tradition and distinguish it from others;
3. Each research tradition (unlike a specific theory) goes through a number of different, detailed (and often mutually contradictory) formulations and generally has a long history extending through a significant period of time. (By contrast, theories are frequently shortlived). (Laudan, 1977, pp. 78–9, italics as in the original).

A research tradition lays down guidelines which shape the development of theories formulated within a particular research tradition. These guidelines exist mainly in two areas: firstly, the scope of the research tradition will be indicated – this basically refers to the 'domain' in which the theories of the research tradition are considered to be most applicable. Laudan refers to the example of Marxism which would not be feasible without the existence of capitalism and its social relationships.

Secondly, a research tradition normally entails a distinct methodology. There are ways of theorising, testing and dealing with empirical and conceptual problems that are often only undertaken by members of a particular research tradition. This is an important point because, as we shall see in Chapters 7 and 8, Austrians and Marxists are distinguished very much by the methodologies they employ.

These two guidelines are designed to indicate to the adherents of any research tradition what they can and cannot do. If practitioners break with either the metaphysics or methodology of a research tradition they effectively repudiate it. If any Keynesian suddenly states that aggregate demand is not a significant determinant of national income and that macroeconomic stabilisation policy is ineffective then they would have effectively repudiated part of their metaphysical commitment to the Keynesian research tradition. If an Austrian economist argues in favour of the use of large-scale macroeconometric forecasting models this will constitute a serious rejection of the anti-empiricist methodology associated with that research tradition (a point that will become clearer in the course of Chapter 7).

There are obvious similarities with Kuhn and Lakatos. Kuhn makes much of exemplary theories – it is their success that attracts new adherents to an emerging paradigm, also the metaphysical commitment is very similar to Lakatos' notion of the hard core. In addition, the research tradition, as with paradigms and research programmes, is intended to aid the corporate activity of the scientific community in their advance towards progress. As with Kuhn and Lakatos, Laudan is suggesting that there can be no science, or, at least, scientific progress, without a research tradition to stimulate scientific activity.

However, there are also differences. Laudan sees his notion of research traditions as being both more flexible and more realistic than the notions of Kuhn and Lakatos. For example, it is quite feasible for different theories within a developing research tradition to be rivals. This should not necessarily be taken as a sign of crisis, as it would with Kuhn. Rather, it is often an indication of scientists within a particular tradition working towards the elimination of different theories in their attempts to make them testable. The research tradition itself is not testable. What testability there is within a research tradition relates to its component theories.

Actually Laudan emphasises that when a research tradition is rejected, largely because of the burden of empirical and conceptual problems weighing it down or because the alternative tradition's problem-solving effectiveness proves more powerful, such a judgement can only be tentative, that is, it is quite possible that we may return to a discredited research tradition at a later date. This is something that Kuhn would never sanction. However, it is one of the features that makes Laudan's work more relevant for economists.

The 'abandoning' of research traditions, with a subsequent revival of its fortunes, is not an uncommon phenomenon within economics. The emphasis upon problems should make this a possibility. Empirical and conceptual problems are frequently emerging, making life difficult, but interesting, for different economic research traditions: a problem solved in one decade may be undone in the next, Keynesianism and its conceptual explanation of employment being one example. Also a perspective that was deemed unsatisfactory in one situation may prove more capable of dealing with different situations.

The case of the Austrians is illustrative of this. In the 1930s this group of economists consistently argued against government intervention to cure the depression of that time. They actually argued that it was government intervention, especially an excessively restrictive monetary policy in the USA, which had been one of the most notable causes of the depression. However, Keynes' message prevailed, government intervention in economic affairs became respectable and the Austrians were eclipsed. However, the fortunes of the Austrians have experienced a dramatic revival in recent years and the Keynesian consensus has now broken down: this has led many to re-evaluate the extent of government intervention in economic affairs. Also macroeconometric modelling and forecasting has increasingly been called into question. The doubts expressed by Austrians on this have now been seen to possess more validity. Furthermore, the emphasis placed upon uncertainty and expectations has made the Austrian view of economic instability more attractive to increasing numbers.

Laudan talks more in terms of evolutionary changes, rather than dramatic breaks, in research traditions. He suggests that the areas most susceptible to change within any research tradition are subsidiary theories that are frequently being modified. The allegiance that adherents to a tradition have means that they are usually more willing to dispense with particular theories than the research tradition itself. This helps to explain the rapid turnover of theories. This phenomenon clearly operates within economics.

Let us take the neo-classical research tradition to be exemplified by the concepts of utility and profit-maximising individuals and firms: that is, the concept of maximising behaviour is a metaphysical commitment. Within the context of the theory of the firm, perfect competition has frequently been criticised as being unrealistic and irrelevant in the context of a mature industrial economy and partly in response to this a succession of theories of oligopoly emerged. From Cournot's duopoly model of the last century to the kinked demand curve, through to various price-leadership and cost-plus theories of oligopoly behaviour (see Koutsoyiannis, 1979, chs 9–14). A similar story can be told in the context of consumer theory (see Koutsoyiannis, 1979, ch. 2; and Green, 1976). What most of these developments have in common is that they can still be accommodated within the framework of maximising behaviour. Therefore, neo-classical economists have generally felt quite happy to develop such theories.

However, when the basic assumptions of a research tradition are threatened this will pose a serious challenge to it and if the neo-classical model was forced to dispense with the maximising postulate this would be a serious blow. Its generality and simplicity would be reduced; also, important methodological implications would follow. The assumption of maximising behaviour enables neo-classical economists to employ mathematical techniques such as differential calculus, along with Lagrange Multipliers, to good effect in analysing the response of consumers and producers to changes in their circumstances. The removal of the maximising postulate would, at a stroke, severely restrict the application of differential calculus to consumer and production theory. Also, many of the 'neat' solutions to mathematical problems, largely facilitated by assumptions of rational and maximising behaviour, would be lost.

Therefore, it is not surprising that economists unsympathetic to neo-classical orthodoxy have frequently focused upon maximising behaviour as a target for their attacks. I will refer to this debate, and one methodological response to it, in the next chapter.

Laudan is, therefore, far more cautious than Kuhn when he considers changes in research traditions. Research traditions have a history, and they evolve, so many of the problem-solving devices will be maintained throughout such evolutions. Also certain empirical problems may, broadly, retain their significance. However, a research tradition that has experienced several stages of evolution may have a different domain of application or methodology from its earlier days. For example, Keynesian economists became increasingly dependent upon the use of large-scale econometric models for purposes of prediction and policy formulation. However, Keynes himself had a number of very strong objections to the use of econometrics for such purposes (see Pheby, 1985).

How do we assess alternative research traditions? We can begin by considering the adequacy of a research tradition at a particular moment in time: this will necessitate emphasising the effectiveness of the most recent theories within that tradition for solving problems. An alternative to this procedure would be to consider the overall progressiveness of the tradition. Here the concern is to ascertain whether the research tradition has increased or decreased in its effectiveness for solving problems. This necessarily involves some consideration of the history of the research tradition, for it is only within its historical context that we can gauge increases or decreases in its problem-solving capacity.

Laudan also distinguishes between the general progress and the rate of progress of a research tradition. The general progress of a research tradition can be established by comparing the adequacy of the theories which constituted the earlier versions of the tradition with those that form the most recent versions of it. The rate of progress reflects changes in the adequacy of the research tradition at a particular moment, so a research tradition could have made significant progress but currently be in the doldrums.

Such considerations lead Laudan to argue that it is rational to accept one research tradition over another when that tradition has proved itself capable of solving more important problems than its competitors. However, this does seem to beg the question. Laudan wishes to undertake a sort of cost-benefit analysis of solved and unsolved problems, assigning weights to them. Is inflation more serious than unemployment? Such questions are not easily answered.

Laudan has some interesting things to say about *ad hoc* modifications. We have seen how blatant attempts to save a theory in the face of conflicts with the facts were frowned upon by Popper, Kuhn and Lakatos but the views of these methodologists are too severe. To Laudan *ad hoc* modifications are often empirically progressive; the point he is making is that a theory faced with an anomalous phenomenon is, from a purely problem-solving point of view, 'better' once an *ad hoc* modification enables the theory to account for the anomaly. Laudan does not accept that *ad hoc* modifications are necessarily cosmetic; rather, he believes that the resolution of anomalies is often a difficult task that requires much ingenuity. Therefore, if *ad hoc* modifications lead to an increase in the problem-solving capability of a research tradition this is to be welcomed. However, if the *ad hoc* modification decreases the problem-solving effectiveness of the research tradition it is unacceptable.

Laudan's approach has much to say about the way in which we should study the history and sociology of a discipline. We have already seen the important role that consideration of the history of a research tradition can play in the assessment of a research tradition. He argues that any meaningful analysis of the historical development of any research tradition necessarily needs to 'take account of *all* of the "cognitively relevant" factors which were *actually present'* (Laudan, 1977, p. 138, italics as in the original). This includes, for example, theological, political and sociological factors. Such factors frequently affect the way in which scientific work is done, and its character, and it is not irrational to take such factors into consideration.

SCIENTIFIC REVOLUTIONS

I have already noted how Laudan regards change as more evolutionary than revolutionary and he sees many problems in the analysis of scientific revolutions. For example, he argues that their occurrence needs to allow for 'a persistent disharmony among scientists concerning the basic foundations of their discipline', and that there is necessarily a degree of arbitrariness when considering whether a 'sizeable' number of new adherents to an alternative research tradition constitutes a revolution. However, Laudan suggests the following:

> *I am suggesting that a scientific revolution occurs when a research tradition, hitherto unknown to, or ignored by scientists in a given field, reaches a point of development where scientists in the field feel obliged to consider it seriously as a contender for the allegiance of themselves or their colleagues.* (Laudan, 1977, p. 138, italics as in the original)

This is an interesting characterisation of a scientific revolution because it seems more realistic than other formulations previously considered. We do not totally abandon everything we have done. This seems to fit the experience of economics rather well.

In the 1930s Keynes boasted that 'everyone' was engaged in debate over the *General Theory*. This is not to say that everyone actually agreed with him. As mentioned above, many economists such as R. G. Hawtrey, A. C. Pigou, F. A. Hayek and Dennis Robertson did not agree with much of Keynes' work. However, they felt compelled to concentrate much of their intellectual energies on refuting Keynes. To a greater or lesser extent, they were all sucked into undertaking work associated with the Keynesian research tradition.

A more recent example of a 'revolutionary episode' is that of the rise of rational expectations since the early 1970s. There has been an absolute explosion of interest in this area (see Shaw, 1984) and this has resulted in Keynesians, monetarists and Austrians being forced to consider this new challenge, if only to defend themselves. So it does seem that Laudan's definition of a revolution or, more appropriately, revolutionary episodes, is applicable to economics.

However, Laudan reiterates his feelings that we should not get too absorbed with revolutions, as they are the exception rather than the rule – ultimately, a revolution rarely will be decisive and mark the obituary for alternative research traditions. What we are more likely to encounter are research traditions being subject to continuous scrutiny and evaluation and as we have seen, this will always be of a comparative nature. Indeed this process is analogous to guerilla warfare. A particular research tradition may be attacked, and its defences breached, by an élite group from a rival tradition. However, it is not completely destroyed and is afforded some opportunity to regroup and mend its defences with a possible counter-offensive to follow. This characterisation of a war of attrition seems to be a more accurate portrayal of how scientific traditions in economics conduct their activities. Final or ultimate victories are rare!

CRITICISMS OF LAUDAN'S APPROACH

Musgrave (1979, p. 452) summarises the way in which Laudan seeks to assess the effectiveness of alternative research traditions. This would involve counting the number of problems a tradition solves, assigning some weight to the significance of these problems, and thus obtaining a number. A similar procedure would be undertaken with respect to empirical anomalies and conceptual problems. When we have the two numbers we can subtract one from the other in order to assess the overall problem-solving effectiveness of a research tradition. This would actually enable us to compare rationally alternative research traditions. However, as Musgrave points out, Laudan does not actually provide us with a complete example of this. There are lots of historical examples of empirical and conceptual problems, but little guidance as to how we should weight them and arrive at a number.

Musgrave also points out that another crucial limitation of Laudan's approach is his failure to say very much about the individuation of problems. This is a very fundamental point, for if we have no reliable means of identifying problems then discussions concerning their weights and significance are irrelevant.

Musgrave also attacks Laudan's argument that we do not need to search for truth and this poses a serious problem for Laudan. He makes much of how scientists deal with the real problems, rather than pseudo-problems, but how is this distinction made? Presumably we have some notion of truth or falsity with respect to the problems in order to make such judgements. Also, if we are so concerned with the rationality and progressiveness of science, surely this implies some movement towards understanding the real world, and therefore truth? Musgrave feels that this is implicit within Laudan's approach. Indeed conceptual problems are serious largely because they involve inconsistencies. But why are they inconsistent? Partly because they are not true, one suspects.

McMullin (1979, p. 827) queries the notion of the research tradition and poses the question as to when does an evolving research tradition become so transformed that it effectively forms a different tradition. Also, given the rapid changes that can occur, even to core assumptions, it becomes increasingly difficult to identify research traditions. This is important because the problems and their significance we analyse are dependent, to some extent, upon the research tradition within which they arise.

There also seems to be a real sense, as with Lakatos, in which the flexibility of Laudan's model, coupled with some vagueness in identifying key components within it, permits a situation where 'anything goes', but Laudan denies this. Similar and other criticisms of Laudan can be found in Doppelt (1981), Feyerabend (1981), Krips (1980) and Newton-Smith (1981).

However, Laudan never denied that his model was far from perfect and he is refreshingly candid in recognising that much elaboration is still required. Having said this, we have seen that in certain respects Laudan does seem to provide economists with a more flexible model that would seem to be of some value to us. Indeed, his emphasis upon the study of the history and sociology of a subject is one that is increasingly being endorsed by economists and it is to be hoped that his approach will receive more attention from economists.

6 Instrumentalism and Economics

In this chapter I shall outline the methodology of instrumentalism, evaluate it and consider how it relates to methodological discussions within economics, and this will entail some consideration of Milton Friedman's famous, and controversial, essay on economic methodology. Discussion of this essay has been postponed until this chapter for two reasons. Firstly, Friedman's essay is increasingly being interpreted as owing more to instrumentalism than to the positivism implied in its title. Secondly, my earlier discussion of Popper helps to place instrumentalism into sharper relief. Friedman himself has claimed affinities with instrumentalism and Popper, but we shall see that these two perspectives are diametrically opposed. My consideration of instrumentalism will not be confined to Friedman's essay: a growing number of writers are suggesting that much contemporary econometric practice is essentially instrumentalist and I will consider such claims towards the end of the chapter.

INSTRUMENTALISM

Interestingly, Popper has been a long-standing and vociferous critic of instrumentalism. He has also supplied us with a familiar definition of this approach:

> By instrumentalism I mean the doctrine that a scientific theory such as Newton's, or Einstein's, or Schrödinger's should be interpreted as an instrument, *and nothing but an instrument*, for the deduction of predictions of future events (especially measurements) and for other practical applications, and more especially, that a scientific theory should not be interpreted as a genuine attempt to describe certain aspects of our world. The instrumentalist doctrine implies that scientific theories can be more or less efficient, but it denies that they can, like descriptive statements be true or false. (Popper, 1983, pp. 111–12, italics as in the original)

Furthermore, instrumentalists are likely to be very dependent upon a set of 'computation rules' that enable them to perform certain tasks without the need to understand the theory that 'explains' such things. Popper cites examples such as the rules of thumb we apply for calculating exposure times in photography. Also instrumentalists normally are concerned with a particular 'purpose in hand' or domain of applicability.

A similar definition is provided by Hesse (1967):

> Instrumentalists assume that theories have the status of instruments, tools, or calculating devices in relation to observation statements. In this view it is assumed that theories can be used to relate and systematize observation statements and to derive some sets of observation statements (predictions) from other sets (data), but no question of the truth or reference to the theories themselves arise. (p. 407)

This perspective, at first sight, appears to hold certain attractions. Firstly, on the assumption that a separation between theoretical and observation statements is possible, much dispute over conceptual matters concerning alternative perspectives can be avoided. This means that comparisons between different positions can be made using observation statements, that is, by considering how well, or otherwise, each perspective predicts. Tortuous debates over complex conceptual matters and the details of paradigms, hard cores and research traditions can, therefore, be dispensed with.

Secondly, the argument that truth is no longer the central aim of our enquiries is not necessarily as heretical as it first seems. We saw in the last chapter, when discussing Laudan, how the search for truth poses problems for some of the perspectives considered in earlier chapters.

Thirdly, given the improvements in technology, and other devices, predictions have become more accurate in many areas. This enables instrumentalists to make the satisfying claim that by concentrating on predictions, and their accuracy, we are often able to demonstrate that science has made progress.

Fourthly, by ignoring features such as the truth, falsity or validity of theories instrumentalists circumvent the Problem of Induction and difficulties concerning the nature, and specification, of causal relations.

However, instrumentalism has met with a lot of criticism, much coming from Popper. For example, he draws a distinction between the way in which instrumentalists and theoreticians approach their work: theoreticians will endeavour to develop more general theories, whereas instrumentalists will tend to concentrate on the practical purpose in hand. According to Popper, this is a distinction that has important implications.

Firstly, he suggests that instrumentalists are likely to be conservative. An instrumentalist, when faced with two theories that produce similar predictions, will regard such theories as being equally useful. However, theoreticians will not wish to leave things there – they will use theories to explore other situations and possibilities, in order to see where they may be fruitfully applied.

Secondly, Popper believes that instrumentalists fail to distinguish between two uses of prediction. One type of prediction involves the forecasting of anticipated events such as the next appearance of Halley's Comet. The other type of prediction concerns events, or possibilities, that were not anticipated prior to a particular theory, in which that event is entailed, being developed and here we can actually learn of an event from a theory. Such predictions often unearth, to the surprise of their developers, new facts about the world and instrumentalists cannot expect to achieve this by focusing on their type of prediction. For Popper this is an important point. He regards both types of prediction as important when testing theories, but the second type of prediction is more interesting to him as it suggests a bolder approach.

Thirdly, the failure, by instrumentalists, to make questions of truth or falsity the primary concern of their inquiries is anathema to Popper. We have seen how the search for truth is important to him. In Chapter 2 I referred to Popper's commitment to realism which essentially seeks truth. Furthermore, instrumentalists are clearly not going to look for falsifications. Popper regards instumentalism as an unsatisfactory way of 'solving' the Problem of Induction. Indeed he argues that it does nothing of the kind; instead of solving this problem it simply ignores it. We shall see that this does hold implications for those who endeavour to defend Friedman's position.

Fourthly, Popper, as well as others such as Newton-Smith (1981) believe that in science we are primarily interested in *explaining* what is happening in the world. Again, this forms an important part of realist philosophy. Theories cannot explain within an instrumentalist perspective. Indeed, we are unlikely to find any causal narrative accompanying the instrumentalists' predictions and we shall see that this also holds certain implications for econometrics.

Finally, from what I have said so far, it is clear that instrumentalism relies heavily upon the possibility of a separation between observation and theoretical statements. Newton-Smith (1981) raises some pertinent points, and doubts, as to this possibility. This particular point is interesting because it refers back to my earlier discussion of Sir Francis Bacon's inductivism, which has been described as a form of naïve empiricism that promotes 'measurement without theory'. Now instrumentalism is by no means identical to inductivism. However, there are important similarities between these perspectives: the attempt to separate theoretical and observation statements and a strong empirical leaning are features common to both methods. These features are important because they create similar difficulties for both inductivism and instrumentalism, and consequently, despite the widespread criticism and rejection of inductivism within the economics profession, the sort of naïve empiricism identified with that approach, is often a source of complaint when considering econometrics. Having provided some background on instrumentalism we are now in a position to consider Friedman's contribution.

FRIEDMAN'S ESSAY

Friedman's essay 'The Methodology of Positive Economics' has been the source of much debate amongst economists since it appeared in 1953. It would not be claiming too much to say that it is the most cited, if not actually read, work on economic methodology. Before considering the main features of the essay it is necessary to provide some background as to the methodological climate that existed within economics prior to its publication. I have already noted how Terence Hutchison's book *The Significance and Basic Postulates of Economic Theory* (1938) upset several economists with its strong attack on abstract, deductive economics. One of the issues to come out of this debate was the question as to whether the assumptions of economic theory should be more realistic. This debate was partly stimulated by Hall and Hitch (1939) who undertook research into the pricing policies of manufacturing firms which suggested that the assumption of setting prices where marginal costs equal marginal revenues was not only wrong, but also inappropriate. They argued that firms tend to adopt a conventional mark-up above costs when establishing prices. Others, for example Lester (1946), also began to question the realism of such marginalist assumptions.

This encouraged a strong response from certain economists, most notably Machlup (1946) who argued that it does not matter if firms actually do not calculate marginal costs and revenue. What is important is that they act 'as if' they were making such calculations. Such disputes led to something of a *Methodenstreit* in the 1940s as to the realism of assumptions within economic theory. The point about this was that many saw it as a frontal assault upon orthodox neo-classical economic theory and Friedman's essay must be seen as a response to this threat. His contribution not only provides a rationale for employing unrealistic assumptions in economic theory, but also a defence of traditional profit-maximising models of the firm. Friedman begins the essay by outlining the familiar distinction between 'positive' and 'normative' economics. Positive economics is:

> . . . in principle independent of any particular ethical position or normative judgements. As Keynes (John Neville) says, it deals with 'what is', not 'what ought to be'. Its task is to provide a system of generalisations that can be used to make correct predictions about the consequences of any change in circumstances. Its performance is to be judged by the precision, scope and conformity of the predictions it yields. (Friedman, 1953, p. 4).

He regards positive economics as being an 'objective' science akin to those found in the physical sciences. Although economists study more complex phenomena, Friedman believes that the differences between economics and the physical sciences are more ones of degree, rather than kind.

Normative economics is concerned with 'what ought to be', but is not entirely independent of positive economics (see Friedman, 1953, p. 5). At first sight the positive–normative distinction may appear to resemble a demarcation criterion between science and pseudo-science. However, this is not the case – as just noted, positive and normative aspects are frequently interrelated. This is the case when we wish to make 'normative' judgements as to the most appropriate economic policy to pursue and such judgements will always be underpinned by positive economics. Friedman's advocacy of strict monetary control is a good example of this and he argues, normatively, that monetary authorities ought to control the rate of growth of the money supply if they wish to control inflation. However, such advice, as far as Friedman is concerned, is founded upon positive economics which has 'established' the primacy of money supply increases in 'causing' inflation.

I have noted above the way in which the realism of assumptions helped to encourage Friedman to write his essay. What is his position on the realism of assumptions within economics? This is one of the most controversial aspects of his essay. The 'validity' of using particular assumptions is not to be judged by their correspondence with reality. Indeed, attempts to test the accuracy of economic theory by considering the reality of the assumptions employed are largely 'irrelevant' and his attitude on such matters is well captured when he writes:

In so far as a theory can be said to have 'assumptions' at all, and in so far as their 'realism' can be judged independently of the validity of predictions the relation between the significance of a theory and the 'realism' of its assumptions is almost the opposite of that suggested by the view under criticism. Truly important and significant hypotheses will be found to have 'assumptions' that are wildly inaccurate descriptive representations of reality, and in general, the more significant the theory, the more unrealistic the assumptions (in this sense) ... To put this point less paradoxically, the relevant question to ask about the 'assumptions' of a theory is not whether they are descriptively realistic, for they never are, but whether they are sufficiently good approximations for the purpose in hand. And this question can be answered only by seeing whether the theory works which means whether it yields sufficiently accurate predictions. (Friedman, 1953, p. 14)

This is an interesting passage because there is much in it that is highly suggestive of instrumentalism. One implication is that theories are not even attempts to describe reality. Instead they are regarded as instruments by which we can generate predictions. Also, theories are useful more for the 'purpose in hand' than their descriptive reality and furthermore, Friedman's emphasis upon predictions stems also from a typically instrumentalist concern. We saw above how instrumentalists seek a greater degree of consensus by focusing on predictions, that is, observation statements. This is an important aspect of Friedman's essay: he sees positive economics as providing a foundation upon which greater agreement over policy matters can be reached.

Also, there is a hint that Friedman is impatient with detailed discussions over problems of methodology (see Friedman, 1953, p. 43) and consequently he seemingly favours a methodological perspective that circumvents such difficulties. Would this also involve the Problem of Induction?

These considerations are suggestive of an essentially instrumentalist position. However, our attempts to place Friedman's perspective into a coherent framework run into difficulties when we consider his views on testing hypotheses:

As I shall argue at greater length below the only relevant test of the *validity* of a hypothesis is comparison of its predictions with experience. The hypothesis is rejected if its predictions are contradicted ('frequently' or more often than predictions from an alternative hypothesis); it is accepted if its predictions are not contradicted; great confidence is attached to it if it has survived many opportunities for contradiction. Factual evidence can never 'prove' a hypothesis, it can only fail to disprove it, which is what we generally mean when we say, somewhat inexactly, that the hypothesis has been 'confirmed' by experience. (Friedman, 1953, pp. 8–9).

This is quite close to Popper's view of falsification. There we can only reject hypotheses. If a hypothesis is not refuted then it is 'corroborated' rather than confirmed and Friedman seems to be making a similar point. His reference to falsification is by no means isolated and we encounter other references to it (see pp. 23 and 38) – indeed, Friedman met Popper in 1949 and they discussed falsificationism.

We are faced, therefore with an interpretational problem when considering important aspects of Friedman's essay. Some indicators point firmly in an instrumentalist, others in a falsificationist, direction and Friedman has confirmed this by accepting characterisations of his instrumentalism as 'entirely correct', but he also aligned himself with Popper.

Opinions are divided on this question. Boland (1979) has made the strongest assertion that Friedman's essay is instrumentalist, indeed Boland believes that by interpreting the essay in this way it is rendered a coherent methodological work. Furthermore, he feels that Friedman was aware of the Problem of Induction and the difficulties of inductivism more generally and this makes his position quite consistent. Boland argues that the multitude of critics who have taken issue with Friedman have missed this important point and consequently he feels that much of this criticism falls flat. On reading Boland's article it is difficult not to gain the impression that a far greater degree of sophistication and coherence is being attributed to Friedman's position than actually exists. For example, is there anything in the essay that suggests a concern with the Problem of Induction and a means of solving it? It seems a shade fanciful to suggest this. Even if it were we shall see that this would not necessarily be a strong feature of Friedman's position.

Others have also noted an essentially instrumentalist theme within Friedman's essay (for example, Nagel, 1963, p. 218; Caldwell, 1980; and Musgrave 1981). However, these authors, particularly Caldwell, argue that Friedman's position is not entirely instrumentalist. Indeed, as Helm (1984) points out, there are flashes of realism in the essay where Friedman apparently sees theories as being devices not merely for generating predictions, but also for 'explaining' reality.

Several other writers have maintained that Friedman's position owes something to Popper. For example, Blaug (1976) argues that Friedman's position is essentially 'Popper with-a-twist applied to economics' and De Marchi (1976) also shares this conviction. However Agassi (1979), rightly, argues that such Popperian analogies have been taken too far. Although there is a strong suggestion of falsification as a means of testing theories it takes more than this, as we have seen in Chapter 2, to be regarded as a Popperian. For example, is there any trace of a commitment to critical rationalism in the essay? In short, there is not. Indeed, Friedman's general reluctance to respond to critics does not suggest that he takes critical rationalism very seriously. However, more fundamentally, in so far as Friedman's essay contains strong instrumentalist tendencies he will entertain views that are diametrically opposed to those held by Popper. We have seen in the early part of this chapter how Popper regards instrumentalism. It is a perspective that, by not being interested in truth or falsity, cannot lend itself to attempts to falsify theories. As we have seen, it is more concerned with the limits of a theory's applicability. Writers who attempt to place Friedman's essay within a coherent philosophy of science are likely to find this a frustrating, if not futile, exercise: as Helm (1984) has so candidly, and accurately, stated, Friedman's essay is best described as 'muddled and confused'. How else are we to interpret his own claims to be simultaneously linked to both instrumentalism and Popper?

CRITICISMS OF FRIEDMAN'S ESSAY

Criticisms of Friedman's essay have been made for more than thirty years and the secondary literature in this area is now voluminous. Consequently, I will not attempt to systematically consider every critic. This would take too much space, and would also be unnecessary, as many of the criticisms are duplicated. Instead I shall focus on a few of the critics who raise some particularly pertinent points.

In this respect the contribution of Musgrave (1981) is of particular interest. He is a philosopher of science who has worked with both Popper and Lakatos and he makes some very perceptive points about the different roles and status of assumptions within economic theory. He believes that Friedman fails to distinguish between negligibility, domain and heuristic assumptions in economic theory, and argues that Friedman is justified in employing simplifying assumptions. This is something with which few economists would disagree: the important point is the way in which we use these assumptions.

Musgrave begins with a consideration of neglibility assumptions. This is where some factor that we might have expected to affect our analysis has only a negligible effect and consequently it is reasonable to assume that such a factor has no effect upon our analysis. Musgrave refers to an example where we may assume that there is no government. This is not meant literally, rather it refers to the government exerting little effect upon the analysis being undertaken. Musgrave agrees with Friedman when he argues that a hypothesis is important if it 'explains' a lot from a few premises. However, Musgrave disagrees with Friedman's assertion that 'the more significant the theory, the more unrealistic the assumptions' and feels that he is wrong to make a virtue out of hypotheses being 'descriptively false' in their assumptions. Musgrave feels that this goes too far – and believes that Friedman has negligibility assumptions in mind when making such statements.

Domain assumptions are important because they relate to negligibility assumptions in a way which can hold implications for the testability of theories. A domain assumption will usually initially have been a negligibility assumption and as a negligibility assumption it will assert that a particular factor is insignificant to the theory being developed. However, it may transpire that this factor actually *is* important and consequently, if we retain the negligibility assumption it becomes a domain assumption. This means that by holding on to this assumption the domain of applicability, that is, situations where the original negligibility assumption holds, is affected. Musgrave sees this as being an important and subtle distinction. For example, we may assume that the government has a balanced budget. This could mean either that actual unbalanced budgets can be ignored (a neglibility assumption) or it could denote a situation where the theory will only apply in situations of balanced budgets (a domain assumption). Such changes between a negligibility and domain assumption can have significant implications. As Musgrave emphasises, such a change often entails the replacement of a more testable theory with one that is less so. As a result we would have made an *ad hoc* modification in a Popperian sense. Musgrave argues that if we make domain assumptions that are always false this renders the theory resting upon it untestable as the situation posited by the theory will never be encountered. Musgrave (1981) concludes:

So if we value testability, we must hope that our domain assumptions are not always false; indeed, we must hope that they are true of as many situations as possible. Friedman does value testability. But concerning domain assumptions his dictum that 'the more significant the theory, the more unrealistic the assumptions' is precisely the reverse of the truth. The more unrealistic domain assumptions are the less testable and hence less significant is the theory. Contrariwise, the more significant the theory, the more widely applicable it will be. (p. 382)

Therefore, it is evident that we need to consider more carefully the purposes and status of different assumptions. Merely to make a virtue out of the unreality of assumptions is likely to be questionable advice. Indeed, when testing economic theories it may actually prove, as indicated by Musgrave, to be misleading.

Heuristic assumptions are the other type considered by Musgrave. Negligibility assumptions are made in order to rid our theory of *unnecessary* complexity, but heuristic assumptions are made to simplify a theory for purposes of clarity in its early stages so as to eventually arrive at a satisfactory degree of complexity. For example, when constructing a simple Keynesian macroeconomic model we may find it more feasible to begin our analysis by assuming that the economy is closed and that there is no public sector. Having developed the model with reference to the private sector only, that is, consumption and investment, it may then be feasible to relax our assumption concerning the public sector. Therefore we can introduce the public sector into our model and see what the implications for multipliers and other features are. We could then relax the assumption relating to the closed economy and ultimately develop a more complex model. The successive relaxation of these simplifying assumptions is what Musgrave regards as a heuristic device and few economists would deny the value of such procedures. However, this does hold implications for Friedman's insistence on the primacy of prediction in testing theories. When employing heuristic assumptions the theory, at that stage, is not generating the sort of precise predictions that will provide meaningful tests of the theory under construction. Rather, heuristic assumptions represent staging posts on the route towards the generation of such predictions and consequently we need to carefully distinguish between the different statuses of assumptions. Musgrave feels that it is precisely the failure to distinguish between negligibility and domain assumptions that makes Friedman an instrumentalist.

Other critics have focused upon the instrumentalist implications of Friedman's position. Caldwell (1980 and 1982) takes issue with Boland's claim that critics of Friedman's essay have failed to make telling points because they have not appreciated the instrumentalist nature of that work, but we have just seen that this does not apply to Musgrave.

Caldwell makes some general points about instrumentalism: he argues that in so far as Friedman's position can be identified as instrumentalist it is possible to criticise it; and he points out that on methodological grounds if our aim is primarily to develop theories that predict well then instrumentalism is appropriate. This is an obvious, but fundamental point. As Caldwell indicates, and our discussion above demonstrates, if you hold an instrumentalist view this has profound implications for the way in which you approach methodology. Caldwell (1980, p. 371) raises four particular criticisms that can be levelled against instrumentalism.

1. The primacy given to predictions can often lead researchers to look more for statistical correlations than causal explanation, especially when the former perform 'better'. I shall consider this point shortly in the context of contemporary statistical work in economics.
2. It is possible that we can start with false premises and derive true consequences from them. An instrumentalist would not be concerned about this. However, if we want our theories to be true as well as predictively accurate then other forms of theory appraisal, apart from predictive success, will be necessary.
3. As already noted, Popper feels that the instrumentalist position renders theories more or less adequate rather than true or false. Consequently, this means that falsifications are not attempted or attained within this perspective.
4. The unimpressive predictive performance within economics (see Tarascio and Caldwell, 1979) suggests that developing theories that yield accurate predictions is problematic. Furthermore, it raises questions as to the adequacy of much economic theory if appraised solely along such instrumentalist lines.

McLachlan and Swales (1982) take issue with a number of points that arise from Boland's reinterpretation of Friedman's position as being instrumentalist and they argue that instrumentalism does not provide a neat solution to the Problem of Induction. If a theory has predicted well for policy purposes in the past what can instrumentalists claim? They cannot make any inductive inferences about the future performance of the policy because this would land them firmly into the difficulties posed by the Problem of Induction. Furthermore, their lack of causal explanation will leave them unable to convincingly explain why a theory has not performed as expected. Consequently the attractiveness of instrumentalism as a means of solving problems relating to causal relations and induction is only superficial. Let us now consider the implications that an adherence to instrumentalism holds for econometric work.

INSTRUMENTALISM AND ECONOMETRICS

In recent years the use of econometric techniques within economics has been called increasingly into question. What is interesting about this criticism is that some of the writers, both explicitly and implicitly, have identified difficulties that arise from econometricians following an essentially instrumentalist methodology. For example, Blaug (1980) states:

> The journals abound with papers that apply regression analysis to every conceivable economic problem, but it is no secret that success in such endeavours frequently relies on 'cookbook econometrics': express a hypothesis in terms of an equation, estimate a variety of forms for that equation, select the best fit, discard the rest, and then adjust the theoretical argument to rationalize the hypothesis that is being tested. Marshall used to say that scientific explanation is simply 'prediction written backwards'. But the reverse proposition is false: prediction is not necessarily explanation written forwards. Empirical work that fails utterly to discriminate between competing explanations quickly degenerates into a sort of mindless instrumentalism and it is not too much to say that the bulk of empirical work in modern economics is guilty on that score. (pp. 256–7)

Others seem to share this view. For example, Coddington (1972), in an article criticising some of the implications for empirical work to be drawn from Friedman's essay, argues that much statistical work is little more than a form of shallow instrumentalism. Grahl (1977, p. 12) endorses Coddington's views when he states that much econometric work tends 'to degenerate into an extreme pragmatism or "instrumentalism"' and he sees such instrumentalist tendencies as having serious implications. For example, when constructing macroeconometric models we are likely to concentrate more on technical matters of model construction than on theoretical considerations. Consequently we are likely to experience a growing tendency to construct models that are statistically tractable, even if they ignore important conceptual matters such as uncertainty, expectations and economic dynamics. As Grahl puts it, 'it is hardly an exaggeration to say that the result of adopting econometrics as the main investigative technique of economic science has been the divorce of theoretical work from the whole field of measurement and application' (1977, pp. 23–4). Indeed, such an attempt to separate theoretical from observation statements is what we would expect from those practising an instrumentalist methodology. However, Grahl, and he is not alone, sees dangers in such tendencies; he believes that much modelling has become little more than a purely technical exercise with only limited value for 'explaining' what is happening within the economy.

Some writers have commented upon problems of econometric practice without referring specifically to instrumentalism. However, their considerations are relevant, and make more sense, once we place econometrics within an instrumentalist framework. This applies particularly to the question of causality in econometrics. We have seen that part of the appeal of instrumentalism is that it avoids consideration of causal relationships. As noted above this encourages researchers to focus more on correlation than causal connection and as any first year undergraduate will know, these notions of correlation and causation are not synonymous. However, this does not appear to have been appreciated by many econometricians. Black (1982) argues that much econometric work does not adequately distinguish the concepts of correlation and causation. He recognises that if we are to learn things about economics from data we need to make causal inferences, but he is concerned that the language of econometrics tends to subtly translate correlation into causation. For example, the way in which the expressions 'determine', 'influence' and 'predict' are used, although actually referring to correlations, tend to imply 'cause'. He argues that such correlation models should be largely confined to forecasting purposes rather than as a means of interpreting why certain things occur. Zellner (1979) regards the comparative lack of attention by econometricians in considering the concept of causality and to developing suitable tests of causal relations within econometric models as being a particularly serious cause for concern. The implicit adoption of an instrumentalist methodology by many econometricians must take some responsibility for such difficulties arising.

Mayer (1980) is another writer who does not explicitly refer to instrumentalism when criticising econometrics. However, some aspects of his criticisms would be attributed, in part, to the adoption of an instrumentalist outlook amongst econometricians. For example, he feels that the predictive record of many econometric models has been so poor that to use this as a test of theories is virtually meaningless. Also he suggests that much econometrics engages in attempts to secure 'good' t-scores, R^2s and Durbin–Watson statistics. There is a sense in which using such statistics in this way is to use them merely as 'computation rules' in the instrumentalist sense: that is, we tend to place far too much emphasis upon them without conducting other checks, such as a more qualitative consideration of the historical and institutional background to the model.

Thurow (1983) makes several hard-hitting criticisms of the use of econometrics. He, like Mayer, makes the point that econometrics, because of certain technical limitations, can rarely produce reliable or conclusive results. This being the case, instrumentalism cannot deliver the goods within economics in one very important respect. We must remember that one of the central motivating factors behind instrumentalism was the desire, by separating theoretical from observation statements, to enable us to objectively judge, by comparing predictive performances, alternative perspectives. Econometrics, despite its instrumentalist leanings, has not been able to achieve this. Therefore, there is a sense in which we are getting the worst of both worlds when we adhere to instrumentalism. On the one hand it is not acting, using Thurow's apt analogy, as an ice-breaker cutting through the pack of conflicting theories and on the other there is a danger in our ignoring difficult, but important, conceptual matters. We may not be encouraged to develop more complex and sophisticated theories for fear that they may not be statistically tractable.

This failure of instrumentalism within economics has had serious repercussions and has played no small part in econometric work being considered less reputable. Thurow makes a perceptive observation of this development: as statistical work has become less respected it has provided important ammunition for certain deductivist economists and rather than tackle computers economists retreat into a maze of increasing mathematical complexity. Also other deductivists, such as the Austrians, who frown upon the widespread use of statistics within economics, have exploited the current malaise of econometrics and it is to this perspective that I now turn.

7 Austrian Methodology

I now turn to a group of economists known as the Austrians. They form a distinctive paradigm not only for their economic theories, but also for the prominence they have generally given to questions of economic methodology. We shall see that they fall very much into the deductivist strand of methodologists, outlined in Chapter 1. Indeed, many of them openly refer to Jean-Baptiste Say, Nassau Senior, John Elliot Cairnes as important precursors. They have also tended to be highly critical of falsificationist, positivist and instrumentalist methodologies within economics. With increasing doubts being raised over the slavish transference of such methodologies to economics, added to the general revival of interest in economic methodology, it is not surprising that the Austrians' approach has recently received more attention.

In what follows I shall deal in some detail with the methodological views of arguably the major Austrian methodologist, Ludwig von Mises, who held his views very strongly. However, successive Austrians have developed or modified his methodological stance. Consequently a detailed treatment of his views saves us much repetition when I consider contemporary Austrian methodology. I shall then submit Mises' position to criticism and see how some contemporary Austrians such as Ludwig Lachmann, Israel Kirzner, Murray Rothbard and Mario Rizzo have responded to such criticisms. This will then lead us to a particularly interesting feature of this discussion which relates to Popper. Another notable Austrian, Friedrich Hayek, is credited with being a Popperian and if true, this renders his methodological perspective very different from most other Austrians. I will analyse this characterisation and suggest that it is exaggerated, indeed it is more instructive for informing us more precisely about the true relevance of Popper's contribution for economic methodology. In fact, certain important features of Popper's approach were elaborated much earlier by Mises! The chapter will then conclude with a brief assessment of the contribution of Austrian methodology.

LUDWIG VON MISES (1881–1973)

Ludwig von Mises was a student of Friedrich von Wieser and Eugen Böhm-Bawerk, and later knew Carl Menger. These three economists are generally regarded as the founding fathers of the Austrian tradition. Mises worked in the Vienna Chamber of Commerce for some years and wished to take on a teaching job in Vienna University but he was always denied a salaried position there (see Mises, 1978 for much revealing detail on this and many other formative incidents in his intellectual development). This encouraged him to run his famous 'Private Seminar' in the 1920s and early 1930s, in which students from the University were invited to his room at the Chamber of Commerce to discuss issues such as business cycles, capital theory and methodology. Amongst those attending were notable economists such as Fritz Machlup, Friedrich Hayek, Gottfried Haberler, Oskar Morgenstern and Paul Rosenstein-Rodan. He then taught in Geneva from 1934–40 before moving to America in 1940 where he held the position of a Visiting Professor at the Graduate School of Business Adminstration at New York University from 1945–69. Again, as in Vienna, Mises was not an officially salaried professor at New York; he was able to teach there largely because of funding from private foundations. His hatred of Nazism and Marxism and his bitterness at being almost exiled from the academic community of economists strongly influenced his attitudes.

His interests were wide, including politics, law and philosophy. He wrote several books and over two hundred articles. Within economics he is best known for his contribution in three areas. Firstly, it was with his theory of money and the trade cycle that he first made his mark in 1912 with his *Theory of Money and Credit*. Secondly, it was on questions of economic methodology that his attention was increasingly focused: in 1933 he published *Epistemological Problems of Economics* which formed the basis for his mammoth *Human Action: A Treatise On Economics*, first published in English in 1949. This is a quite remarkable work as it develops his distinctive views on methodology and how they relate to virtually all areas of economics. He wrote two other books that specifically dealt with methodology: *Theory and History* (1957) and *The Ultimate Foundation of Economic Science* (1962).

Thirdly, he developed a detailed analysis of the functioning of markets. He was a very committed libertarian and did not favour intervention on the part of government, except for basic things such as law and order. This led him to make many strong criticisms of socialist planning and, later, Keynesian interventionism.

Our focus will necessarily be upon the second of his primary concerns. It is important when discussing Mises' methodology to place it into context. He was a student at the time in which the *Methodenstreit* (conflict over methods) was petering out, that is, the early 1900s. Indeed, he was familiar with this episode from the first-hand accounts he received from one of the main protagonists, Carl Menger. However, Mises did not regard the *Methodenstreit* as over: it could be argued that he contributed significantly to reopening it. Many, including Schmoller, the other main protagonist, who were tired of this dispute rather glibly stated that some combination of induction and deduction was necessary, but Mises did not see things this way – he wanted to emphasise the purely deductive nature of economics. This was for two reasons: firstly, he felt that theoretical considerations were of the utmost importance to economists and by emphasising deduction we would help ensure that this was always borne in mind; secondly, he resented the attempts by economists to imitate the physical sciences. He desperately wanted to preserve the theoretical autonomy of the social sciences and a deductively orientated methodology would go a considerable way towards preventing quantitative techniques, which Mises saw as attempts to ape the natural sciences, from gaining too strong a foothold within economics. How did he endeavour to fulfil such aims?

In *Human Action* he sought to develop a science of human action called *praxeology* (which he originally wanted to call sociology). Praxeology could explain *all* human action, not only that confined to the sphere of economics, but Mises' primary concern was with economics as this was the 'most developed' branch of praxeology.

In order to develop praxeology Mises started with a fundamental axiom which formed the basis of his science of human action:

> Human action is purposeful behaviour. Or we may say: Action is will put into operation and transformed into an agency, is aiming at ends and goals, is the ego's meaningful response to stimuli and to the conditions of its environment, is a person's conscious adjustment to the state of the world that defines his life. (Mises, 1966, p. 11).

The basic axiom is not derived from experience, indeed it is logically prior to it and for Mises this basic axiom was incapable of being proved or disproved. Therefore what stimulates people to act purposefully? A situation of contentment or satisfaction is where we feel no compulsion to act in order to change things. When we are unhappy, or dissatisfied, however, we may act in order to improve our situation. Therefore, action is 'always' encouraged by a feeling of uneasiness and consequently three conditions need to exist before action will be undertaken. The first two are that we have to feel uneasy with our current situation and have a satisfactory alternative in mind and the third condition is that we must have some expectation that our actions will be successful in removing our state of uneasiness. This leads to an important conclusion about, and description of, human action:

> Praxeology is indifferent to the ultimate goals of action. Its findings are valid for all irrespective of the ends aimed at. It is a science of means, not of ends . . . . (Mises, 1966, p. 15)

The means–end distinction is very important to praxeologists. For Mises it helps to explain why all human action is 'necessarily rational', but praxeology can only tell us something about the way people take steps to attain their ends or goals – it does not tell us *why* the individual chooses one end rather than another, and this raises questions as to the *motives* of action that are to be answered by psychologists, not economists.

Praxeologists do not make any value judgements as to the ends chosen by different people. In this sense praxeology claims to be 'positive' – it has something to say about what is, rather than what ought to be. For example, if a group of materially successful people leave their lucrative jobs and establish a hippy commune, such behaviour may well be considered 'irrational' by materialistically-minded people. However, it is the ends of those establishing the commune, not the value judgements of others, which determine whether the hippie's actions are rational or not. If they desire a more healthy, relaxed lifestyle then the commune may be the best means to achieve such ends, therefore to a praxeologist such behaviour is clearly rational.

It is also worth noting that rational behaviour does not preclude actors making mistakes. Too often in neo-classical orthodoxy we assume both rational behaviour and perfect information, but this assumes away an important part of our everyday existence, namely, uncertainty. For the Austrians we live in a complex world where uncertainty prevails. By assuming rationality and perfect information orthodox economists can easily analyse the movement from one state of equilibrium to another, but this does not do justice to the complexities encountered in the real world. Along with uncertainty, the action taken towards substituting a more satisfactory state of affairs for a less satisfactory implies the passage of time and this adds another dimension to Austrian analyses which they feel is inadequately dealt with by orthodox economists. It is simply not enough to flit from one state of equilibrium in the 'short-run' to another in the 'long-run' – market processes are far more subtle and complicated than this suggests. Indeed, we shall see how this type of approach encourages, for Mises, many economists to misuse mathematics. Entrepreneurs, central actors to Austrians, may therefore act rationally but end up broke. If a new venture appears on the information available to be a good prospect it is clearly rational for an entrepreneur to proceed with it. However, if in the next few months demand changes fundamentally, and was unforeseen or some natural disaster destroys his factory an entrepreneur cannot be accused of irrational behaviour in making his initial decision to invest in the venture. There is a sense in which praxeology defines all purposeful behaviour as rational: the example of a young man who wishes to make a favourable impression upon a young woman whom he knows to have an allergy to flowers would simply not be acting purposively in sending her flowers. It is therefore clear that almost any behaviour can be categorised as rational, even whims. If I set out to buy a suit and buy a piece of furniture instead on the way all I have done is to subsitute one end for another.

An important category that needs to supplement the praxeologists framework is that of causality. The acting man needs to be able to discern causal relationships. Means and ends presuppose cause and effect. Indeed, if causality and regularity did not exist then human action and reasoning would be impossible, as chaos would reign. We need to have knowledge of causal relationships otherwise we will not know what action to take in order to attain our desired ends.

It is now clear how fundamentally *a prioristic* and deductive Mises' system is. For Mises, we need to reason *a prioristically* in order to render the complex phenomena of human action intelligible:

> Cognition from purely deductive reasoning is also creative and opens our mind to previously barred spheres. The significant task of *a prioristic* reasoning is on the one hand to bring into relief all that is implied in the categories, concepts and premises, and, on the other hand, to show what they do not imply. It is its vocation to render manifest and obvious what was hidden and unknown before. (Mises, 1966, p. 38)

Indeed, experience cannot prove or disprove our theories. Where contradiction occurs between what our theories imply and our experience we must first check that our deductions have been carried through correctly. Mises (1976, p. 27) argues that 'New experience can force us to discard or modify inferences we have drawn from previous experience. But no kind of experience can ever force us to discard or modify *a priori* theorems.'

I need to say a few words at this point about the belief of Mises, and most other Austrians, in methodological individualism and subjectivism.

Methodological individualism and subjectivism within Austrian methodology are intimately connected. Methodological individualism is well summarised in these classic statements from Watkins (1968):

> The ultimate constituents of the social world are individual people who act more or less appropriately in the light of their dispositions and understanding of their situation. Every complex social situation, institution or event is the result of a particular configuration of individuals, their dispositions, situations, beliefs and physical resources and environment. These may be unfinished or half-way explanations of large-scale social phenomena (say, inflation) in terms of other large-scale phenomena (say, full employment): but we shall not have arrived at rock-bottom explanations of large-scale phenomena until we have deduced an account of them from statements about the dispositions, beliefs, resources and inter-relations of individuals. (pp. 270–1)

He describes the central assumption of methodological individualism in the following terms:

> No social tendency exists which could not be altered if the individuals concerned both wanted to alter it and possessed the appropriate information. (They might want to alter the tendency but, through ignorance of the facts and/or failure to work out some of the implications of their actions, fail to alter it, or perhaps even intensify it). (Watkins, 1968, p. 271)

Therefore, methodological individualists argue that it is only individuals who possess aims and objectives. Methodological individualists regard collective terms such as 'the working class' or 'the consumption function' with great suspicion. This clearly has implications for Austrians' views on macroeconomic aggregates: these will play a far less meaningful role in their analyses. Indeed the primacy given to individuals as actors is a clear indication of how much Austrians will differ from Keynesians, who are much happier to deal with aggregate functions.

The praxeological nature of methodological individualism is also evident when we see, from the above quote, how the methodological individualist notion of rationality emphasises purposeful behaviour. They argue that individuals behave in ways which are adequate for their purposes. Methodological individualists recognise, as in the case of our entrepreneur, that human actors will not always achieve their purpose, due to insufficient information, bad luck or whatever.

The other key aspect associated with methodological individualism is that changes in the institutions of society occur primarily through the actions of individuals. They reject theories of change that argue that some 'spirit of the age' or 'climate of the times' somehow imposes itself upon society from above. Climates and spirits are created by the individuals within that society.

Subjectivism is best regarded as one way in which methodological individualists can proceed with their analyses. Subjectivists argue that economics is essentially a science concerned with the purposeful action of individuals. This means that in such analyses the intentions of these acting individuals are of primary importance. The question is, how can we obtain insights into the intentions of other individuals? Subjectivists proceed by looking to their own thoughts when placed in a similar situation to that of the individual they are considering, the assumption being that our own thoughts on the matter will provide us with some insight as to how others will behave. Subjectivists feel that this is a reasonable way to approach the study of individual action. They believe that it is possible to make 'pattern' predictions as to how people will behave under certain circumstances. For example, if a roomful of people smell smoke nearby it is likely that most of them will run for the nearest exit.

It is clear that adherence to such positions is likely to place Austrians firmly against Marxism and Keynesianism. We shall see shortly how methodological individualism holds relevance for the connection of Popper's philosophy with economic methodology.

Mises sought to emphasise the desire to render human action intelligible and understandable. Testing, prediction and control were not important parts of his programme and it is, therefore, not surprising that he saw only a limited role for quantitative analysis within economics. His primary objection to the deployment of statistical techniques was the lack of constant relationships within economics. If we do not accept the possibility of constant relationships then prediction and control become impossible. Let us consider two examples where a belief in constant relationships can prove misleading.

Firstly, Mises refers to the Quantity Theory of Money. In its 'naïve' form it is argued that the general price level will change proportionately to the change in the money supply. This is fallacious according to most Austrians and Mises did much to develop the Austrian view on money and prices. This theory accepts that changes in the money supply affect prices throughout the economy. However such price changes will vary considerably in different sectors of the economy and the very complexity of the economy means that different market conditions prevail and consumers and investors will respond differently to the change in the money supply. If we experience an increase in the money supply this could result in a reduction in interest rates and make credit both easier and cheaper. Therefore certain markets that are more dependent on consumer credit may experience a sharper increase in prices, especially if a situation of excess demand already exists, and other markets may have such a glut that price reductions are witnessed. The point is that the Quantity Theory of Money cannot provide us with any precise predictions as to price changes in different markets.

Secondly, Mises considers the example of the estimation of demand functions, a particularly popular early application of econometric techniques. If we establish that a 10 per cent increase in the supply of potatoes at a particular time, resulted in an 8 per cent reduction in their price, this tells us something about the elasticity of demand for potatoes. However, it can only tell us something specific in terms of a market at one particular time; it cannot provide us with any indication as to what is likely to happen in the future. Indeed, for Mises, the primary, and legitimate, role for quantitative work came in its analysis of past historical situations. Man's behaviour with respect to potatoes, as with many other goods and services, will change, therefore when we have no constant relationships we cannot have any meaningful measurement.

Acting man is necessarily looking to the future and the uncertainties implied in such speculative activities. No amount of quantitative analysis can hope to cast any light on such phenomena. The very nature of praxeological man is such that we should not look to the external world with a view to observing it:

> Praxeology does not deal with the external world, but with man's conduct with regard to it. Praxeological reality is not the physical universe, but men's conscious reaction to the given status of this universe. Economics is not about men, their meanings and actions. Goods, commodities and wealth and all other notions of conduct are not elements of nature; they are elements of human meaning and conduct. He who wants to deal with them must not look to the external world; he must search for them in the meaning of acting man. (Mises, 1966, p. 92)

This last statement is further confirmation of Mises' rejection of positivistic and instrumentalist methodologies for economics. Apart from the lack of constant relationships within economics, Mises was also very aware of the difficulties associated with probability and induction in quantitative work: his brother, Richard, was a famous probability theorist.

For Mises something is probable if our knowledge of it is deficient. However, praxeologists cannot turn to the frequency theory of probability for any assistance. The very nature of the frequency theory is that we require groups of phenomena – Mises calls them 'classes' – from which we can obtain frequencies. However, for praxeologists it is individual actions that are the centre of attention. Individuals have different reasons, that is, ends and goals, for acting as they do and consequently it is misleading to bring them all together as if they define a distinct class of phenomena: 'Every action is speculative. There is in the course of human events no stability and no safety' (Mises, 1966, p. 113). If one accepts this then the usefulness of the frequency theory of probability within economics is severely limited.

Related to his doubts over probability are his reservations over the use of induction (see, for example, Mises, 1962, pp. 21–7). He realised the significance of the Problem of Induction for quantitative work, indeed he echoed the arguments already made in Chapter 1 that this fundamental problem imposes severe limitations on what we can do with quantitative work in economics. He argued that invocation of the Principle of the Uniformity of Nature is an inadequate and invalid response on the part of those who wish to employ induction for purposes of predicting future events. Mises also thought that probability theory was an inappropriate way of dealing with inductive problems.

That Mises should have held such strong views is understandable. We must recall that he disliked attempts on the part of economists to ape the physical sciences and did not believe that the *Methodenstreit* was over. These points help to explain the vehemence with which he criticised and rejected the use of much mathematical economics and econometrics.

Indeed, on top of his doubts expressed over the lack of constancy in economic relationships, induction and probability Mises saw in the rise of econometric techniques another manifestation of the naïve inductivism associated with the German Historical School. We need to bear in mind that during the 1940s, when his *Human Action* was being prepared, econometrics was beginning to make an impact within the economics profession. However, for Mises, econometrics was often a crude, and naïve, form of inductivism. If this approach became too dominant it would do much to damage the theoretical side of economics. Over the years Mises' attitude against econometrics hardened – in *The Ultimate Foundation of Economic Science* (1962) we read of the 'mischief' of modelling economics upon the natural sciences.

Also 'all varieties' of mathematical economics and 'especially econometrics' are 'fundamentally fallacious'. In fact, econometrics is summarily dismissed as 'childish play with figures that does not contribute anything to the elucidation of economic reality' (Mises, 1962, p. 63).

These sentiments must also be linked with his libertarianism. As econometrics developed, particularly in the wake of the Keynesian revolution, large-scale macroeconometric modelling became possible. This played no small part in the belief of governments that they could 'fine-tune' the economy due to the 'insights' provided by such models and Mises undoubtedly recognised econometrics lending itself to such developments.

As for mathematical economics, Mises was scarcely more generous:

> The mathematical method must be rejected not only on account of its barrenness. It is an entirely vicious method starting from false assumptions and leading to fallacious inferences. Its syllogisms are not only sterile; they divert the mind from study of the real problems and distort the relations between the various phenomena. (Mises, 1966, p. 350)

Mises was unhappy with the way in which algebra and geometry were frequently used to represent economic phenomena. As noted above, market processes are complex and for Mises mathematical economics abstracted from such complexities in a way that bore little relation to reality.

Not only econometrics, mathematics, positivism and instrumentalism, but also falsificationism comes in for criticism from Mises. It should by now be clear that Mises' '*a priorism*' is not susceptible to falsification. Indeed, he later explicitly addressed himself to Popper. He dismisses Popper's demarcation criterion that anything that is unfalsifiable in principle is unscientific as 'merely a verbal quibble. No serious man wastes his time in discussing such a terminological question' (Mises, 1962, p. 62). Not surprisingly, these views on economic methodology have elicited some sharp reactions.

CRITICISMS AND REACTIONS TO MISES

Mises views on methodology, though occasionally discussed, have rarely been systematically criticised. A good example of the dismissive attitude is to be found in Blaug (1980, p. 93) who regards Mises' methodological writings as 'so cranky and idiosyncratic that we can only wonder that they have been taken seriously by anyone', but no attempt is made to explain why Mises' method should be so characterised. Many other books on methodology, if they bother to mention Mises, deal only in the most cursory fashion with praxeology. However, there are exceptions to this general trend.

One of the more systematic critiques of praxeology is to be found in Gutiérrez (1971). His central argument is levelled against the 'extraordinary claim' of praxeologists that they can understand reality by employing an *a priori* method. He states his objection to this in the following terms: if praxeology is *a priori* it can have nothing to do with reality; conversely, if it has anything to do with reality, the uniqueness of praxeology, its *a priori* nature, vanishes. This is an important point because it clearly implies that if praxeology is to inform us of reality some form of empirical analysis is required and given Mises' strong strictures on empiricism this poses a dilemma for praxeologists. Either they stick rigidly to their *a priori* stance and consequently run the risk of telling us little about reality, or they endeavour to inform us about reality, and employ some form of empirical analysis. For praxeologists to opt for the first choice would understandably make it unappealing for most economists, but the adoption of the second point implies some accommodation with empiricism. We shall see how some Austrians have handled this.

Block (1973) replied to Gutiérrez's central point by arguing that because a system of thought is *a priori* it does not necessarily mean that it cannot tell us anything about reality. He refers to the example of mathematics, which is clearly *a priori*, but, few would deny that mathematics can be helpful in understanding reality. Block is right in making this point, yet it is an inadequate answer to Gutiérrez's central point. Mathematics can be formulated in such a way that it permits us to derive testable implications – praxeologists do not claim this for their system. Indeed, both Klant (1984, pp. 71–6) and Caldwell (1984) regard this as a weakness of praxeology.

Harwood (1955) has made a similar point when he states:

As for von Mises' assertion that economists must rely on 'cognition and analysis of our own purposeful behaviour', this is the thoroughly discredited mode of knowing by introspection. Moreover, how can even the method of introspection be used if the knowledge praxeology provides is '*a priori*', i.e. 'not subject to verification or falsification on the ground of experience and facts?' If we find neither experience nor facts when we 'analyse our own purposeful behaviour', do we find anything at all? (p. 40)

Indeed, Harwood perceptively notes a couple of instances (p. 41) where Mises employs facts to analyse certain economic relationships!

Caldwell (1984), in characteristically judicious fashion, raises several pertinent points concerning praxeology. He points out that it is inadequate to accuse Austrians, as does Hutchison (1981), of dogmatism in their advocacy of '*a priorism*'. This is because such criticisms are frequently dogmatic themselves. He also points out that it is not sufficient to place too much emphasis upon the unfalsifiable nature of the basic action axiom of purposeful behaviour. He points out that the central neo-classical axiom of profit-maximising behaviour can also be criticised in this way. Indeed, many of the critics have tended to show their dislike of praxeology from positivistic, instrumentalist and falsificationist perspectives. As we have seen in preceding chapters these methodologies suffer from severe difficulties of their own and it is, therefore, a dubious practice to judge praxeology against standards which are themselves so questionable. Indeed, it needs to be recognised that Mises made a number of telling criticisms against many modern methodologies. Caldwell argues that a meaningful criticism of praxeology needs to consider the nature of the axioms and he refers particularly to the need for a close look at the status of the secondary axioms.

The extreme '*a priorism*' of Mises does encounter problems when we consider these secondary or subsidiary axioms of praxeology and there appears to be little agreement as to just how many of these we should employ. This is an interesting point because it raises an issue that is analogous to that encountered in Chapter 4 over the definitional difficulties of distinguishing between hard-core, non-falsifiable, axioms and assumptions, and those of the protective belt, which are susceptible to falsifiability. Rizzo (1982) implicitly recognises this when he attempts to recast Austrian methodology in Lakatosian terms – this way an '*a prioristic*' hard core can be preserved, with a degree of flexibility, and testability, injected into the methodological proceedings.

Mises himself recognised that the economy changes and consequently, institutional structures, whether markets or governments, change over time. It seems clear that Austrians will necessarily need to make some periodic adjustments to their secondary assumptions if they are to render economic phenomena intelligible and Rothbard (1976), a confirmed praxeologist, seems to realise this. He regards the praxeological axioms as being 'broadly empirical', rather than purely *a priori*. Other praxeologists, whilst accepting many of Mises' central tenets, differ on certain points. Lachmann (1970 and 1977) leaves us in little doubt as to his essentially praxeological methodology. However, in Lachmann (1982) an argument is presented which criticises Mises' use of subjectivism. Lachmann argues that Mises employed a restrictive form of subjectivism that tended to analyse ends as if they were given. This contributed to Mises ignoring the complex problem of expectations, something that most Austrians regard as vital in their work. O'Driscoll and Rizzo (1985, p. 23) have made a similar point – they argue that Mises practised a form of subjectivism that was static. This form of subjectivism is essentially deterministic and mechanistic, indeed it is based upon classical mechanics. This is a serious charge on two counts. Firstly, it suggests that Mises' approach is perhaps not that different from some of the 'naturalistic' methodologies that he was so fond of attacking. The second, and I believe more serious difficulty, is that Mises' approach is unable to deal satisfactorily with the dynamism, complexity and openness of the real world.

The methodological individualism of Mises and other Austrians has also been criticised. The most interesting criticism refers to the role that institutions play in influencing the behaviour of individuals. It is clear from the above citation that Watkins recognises that institutions are relevant, a fact that Mises (1966, p. 45) also appreciates. Some critics (for example, Goldstein, 1951) argue that methodological individualists have great difficulty in analysing the interaction between individuals and institutions. Goldstein sees this as the central weakness of methodological individualism – what is lacking is a systematic theory of institutions and institutional change and this is necessary in order to lend greater credibility to the methodological individualists programme. This is a demanding task which few Austrians have been prepared to tackle, Lachmann (1970) being a notable exception, yet it is an aspect of Austrian methodology that requires greater attention. Kirzner (1976) is another Austrian who talks a lot about praxeology. According to Caldwell (1984, p. 363) he has a more relaxed view as to the *a prioristic* nature and logical structure of axioms.

Rothbard and Kirzner were both students of Mises and the latter's influence has left its mark on the development of Austrian thought, even if many have felt inclined to move away from the position held by Mises. I have already noted how Rizzo seeks a more flexible approach by adopting a Lakatosian framework and more recently he has been party to a work (O'Driscoll and Rizzo, 1985) that is happy to refer to quite high-powered econometric work in order to *test* certain Austrian theories. Spadaro (1978) believes that some role for mathematics definitely exists for Austrian economists. He also believes that probabilistic inferences employing subjective notions of probability, rather than frequency probabilities, should be developed by Austrians. Finally, he sees a much wider role for interdisciplinary collaboration with other social scientists.

However, the most dramatic rejection of Mises methodology seemingly comes with the methodological pronouncements of one of his former students, Friedrich Hayek. He has made statements that suggest his position to be essentially Popperian and this is interesting for two reasons: firstly, it suggests that a very prominent Austrian has broken fundamentally with Mises; and secondly, it raises the issue of how Popper relates to economic methodology. I shall consider both of these points in turn.

The idea of Hayek splitting methodologically with Mises has been strongly advocated by Hutchison (1981). It should be remembered from earlier chapters that Hutchison was particularly distressed by the dominance of '*a priorism*' in economics in the 1930s and he singled out Mises and Robbins as being particularly responsible for this development. They were the primary targets of his *The Significance and Basic Postulates of Economic Theory* (1938). We have seen how he advocated a combination of falsificationism and positivism for economists and it is not surprising that he should seize an opportunity to 'rescue' Hayek, an economist he respects, from the *a prioristic* clutches of Mises. Hutchison argues that we can identify, methodologically, Hayek I and II. Hayek I, essentially in the Misesian mould existed prior to 1937; after this date Hayek II emerges – he is someone who sees a definite role for falsificationism within economics and does not seem to be as paranoid as Mises about employing some of the techniques of the natural sciences. Is this fundamental split actually valid? Caldwell (1985) has examined Hutchison's claims closely and argues that they are largely unfounded.

There are two key issues involved here. Firstly, how far did Hayek really embrace Popper? Secondly, did Hayek totally reject his 'Misesian' heritage? When we consider both of these questions it is apparent that the dichotomy between Hayek I and II is false.

Let us consider the linkages with Popper. It should be emphasised that Hayek and Popper have been close friends for many years. Consequently Hayek has certainly had plenty of exposure to Popper's methodological views. This shows in his writings where falsificationism is something that is increasingly referred to.

For example, in the essay 'Degrees of Explanation' (Hayek, 1967, pp. 4–5) he outlines some key features of Popper's system which eschew the use of induction and endeavour to falsify theories rather than verify them. These arguments are 'accepted' by Hayek. Elsewhere we encounter other favourable references to Popper. In his essay 'The Pretence of Knowledge' (Hayek, 1978) he endorses Popper's demarcation criteria in the following terms:

> We cannot be grateful enough to such modern philosophers of science as Sir Karl Popper for giving us a tool by which we can distinguish between what we may accept as scientific and what not – a test which I am sure some doctrines widely accepted as scientific would not pass. . . . (pp. 31–2)

Later in the same piece, after much qualification as to the preciseness of prediction within the social sciences he states: 'Yet, as I am anxious to repeat, we will still achieve predictions which can be falsified and which therefore are of empirical significance' (p. 33).

At first sight, then, it seems as if Hutchison's claim that Hayek was a convert to Popperianism is valid. However, the 'conversion' should not be exaggerated – when we read other extracts from Hayek his 'falsificationism' is so heavily qualified as to weaken it considerably. For example, when discussing 'complex phenomena', which relates to the social sciences, he argues:

> The advance of science will thus have to proceed in two different directions; while it is certainly desirable to make our theories as falsifiable as possible, we must also push forward into fields where, as we advance, the degree of falsifiability necessarily decreases. This is the price we have to pay for an advance into the field of complex phenomena'. (Hayek, 1967, p. 29)

It seems that Hayek, like many other economists, has been seduced into adopting falsificationist rhetoric. We saw in Chapter 2 that there was much more to Popper than mere falsificationism and it was argued that critical rationalism is a particularly important feature of Popper's methodology. My own reading of Hayek does not leave the impression of someone who is particularly strongly endowed with this methodological faculty.

None of this should be surprising when we tackle the Hayek I and II dichotomy from the second perspective – Mises' connection. The argument of Hutchison is that Hayek's Popperian break with Mises came in 1937. This is not only unfounded, but incorrect. In Hayek's

(1980) 'The Facts of the Social Sciences' we encounter some very Misesian themes:

> All that the theory of the social sciences attempts is to provide a technique of reasoning which assists us in connecting individual facts. It can, therefore and this is the second point, never be verified or falsified by reference to facts. All that we can and must verify is the presence of our assumptions in the particular case . . . But the theory itself, the mental scheme for the interpretation, can never be 'verified' but only tested for its consistency. It may be irrelevant because it does not take account of a sufficient number of conditions. But it can no more be disproved by facts than can logic or mathematics. (p. 73)

This was first published in 1943 and seems sufficiently 'Misesian' to render Hutchison's 1937 dichotomisation of Hayek I and II groundless. Furthermore, Hutchison does not refer to Hayek's *The Counter-Revolution of Science* (1979). Although begun in the early 1940s it was not completed until the late 1950s. It is interesting that Hayek intimates (p. 45) that he did not care much for the expression 'praxeology'. However the whole work is concerned with purposeful human action designed to achieve certain ends and is a strong refutation of 'scientism' (attempts by social scientists to ape the natural sciences). Are not these two of the most fundamental features of Mises' work?

Hayek's 'Misesian' lineage is found in his more recent work. In 'The Theory of Complex Pheonomena' (Hayek, 1967) he makes many criticisms of quantitative work in the social sciences and emphasises the difficulties posed by a lack of constancy in economic relationships and the limitations of the frequency theory of probability. Hayek has also warned that too much attention being paid to statistical work could easily lead to a disregard for important theoretical considerations. Indeed, in 'The Pretence of Knowledge' Hayek argued that Mises' anxieties concerning the aping of the natural sciences and the desire to predict and control that this encouraged were justified. Recall how Mises saw the justification for increased interventionism resulting from this. Hayek cites Keynesian interventionism as being erroneous and that such policies were 'a direct consequence of this scientistic error' of believing that we can employ natural science techniques in order to control economic affairs:

> The theory which has been guiding monetary and financial policy during the last thirty years, and which I contend is largely the product

of such a mistaken conception of the proper scientific procedure, consists in the assertion that there exists a simple positive correlation between total employment and the size of the aggregate demand for goods and services; it leads to the belief that we can permanently assure full employment by maintaining total money expenditure at an appropriate level. Among the various theories advanced to account for extensive unemployment, this is probably the only one in support of which strong quantitative evidence can be adduced. I nevertheless regard it as fundamentally false, and to act upon it, as we now experience, as very harmful. (Hayek, 1978, pp. 23–4)

Böhm (1985) has informed me that in conversations he had with Hayek, the latter has stated firmly that he was *never* a fully-fledged praxeologist. It is true that Hayek did not advocate *a priorism* in the strident manner of Mises, and he also saw a larger role for mathematical economics than Mises ever did. However, when all things are considered Hayek retained many of the fundamental attitudes held by Mises. Taken together such attitudes form a distinctive approach toward economics that is clearly out of sympathy with many of the current trends within economics.

I can now turn to a brief consideration of Popper's relevance to economic methodology as it is linked with aspects of our discussion of Austrian methodology. Popper was never an *a priorist*, but he does hold some methodological perspectives in common with the Austrians. Popper's major work on the methodology of the social sciences is *The Poverty of Historicism* (1976b). In this work Popper is conscious of the dangers of social scientists trying to emulate the natural sciences and this is particularly serious when we consider historicism. He defines this as 'an approach to the social sciences which assumes that *historical prediction* is their principal aim, and which assumes that this aim is attainable by discovery of the "rhythms" or the "patterns", the "laws" or the "trends" that underlie the evolution of history' (Popper, 1976b, p. 3). This, for Popper, has exerted a particularly harmful influence upon the social sciences. His particular target, if our discussion in Chapter 2 is recalled, is Marxism. He regards Marxists as being 'historicists' who typically wish to argue deterministically that, for example, the days of capitalism are numbered. We shall see in the next chapter that this is a rather crude interpretation of Marx. Popper's reaction to historicism is to advocate methodological individualism as the most appropriate method for the social sciences. Consequently, this leads him to reject central planning, but not all government intervention, along lines very similar to those of the Austrians. Indeed, he frequently cites Hayek in these connections. Once we go down the road of methodological individualism this also has implications for quantitative analysis. Indeed Popper has some interesting things to say with regard to statistical work in economics. Whilst advocating the use of statistics and mathematics, where appropriate, he states:

> In physics, for example, the parameters of our equations can, in principle, be reduced to a small number of natural constants – a reduction which has been successfully carried out in many important cases. This is not so in economics; here the parameters are themselves in the most important cases quickly changing variables. This clearly reduces the significance, interpretability, and testability of our measurements. (Popper, 1976b, p. 143)

Elsewhere Popper (1983, pp. 7–8) 'dislikes' attempts by those outside the physical sciences to 'ape' the mathematical and statistical techniques used there. Indeed it is probably a more accurate portrayal of developments to argue that Popper was more strongly influenced by Hayek, than vice versa. Some of Hayek's essays, in *The Counter-Revolution of Science* (1979), were first published in the 1940s. It seems that these acted as a strong influence on Popper when writing his *Poverty of Historicism* (1976b). Caldwell (1985) has made this point very persuasively, but I believe that we could go one stage further back and claim some indirect influence from Mises! He was berating historicists and advocating methodological individualism long before Popper. He raised questions about the use of mathematics and statistics that have been echoed, in an admittedly diluted form, by Popper. There is much in Mises that Popper would find repugnant, but their methodological stance towards the social sciences are broadly similar and it is in this context that Popper's methodology is best viewed by economists. It should not be interpreted as the 'naturalistic' methodology outlined in Chapter 2, but a deductive, methodological individualistic approach with a limited role for mathematics and econometrics.

In conclusion, we have seen that Mises' *a priorism* goes too far. However, this is no excuse for denying the many perceptive criticisms that he made regarding the transfer of natural science techniques too slavishly to economics. As we have seen, the lessons learnt when considering positivism, falsificationism and instrumentalism actually render Mises, position less extreme than early interpretations gave him credit for. However, the Younger School of Austrians are wise to attempt some integration with mathematical and econometric techniques. That such techniques have been over-used, if not abused, does not preclude their more balanced application towards the study of complex economic phenomena.

8   Marx's Method

I now turn to consider a very distinctive methodological approach towards the study of economics. Karl Marx's method provides something of an alternative to the methodologies based upon the natural sciences considered above, but writing about Marx's methodology is problematic and this is largely due to his failure to leave us any systematic treatment of his method. This has encouraged a number of contrasting characterisations of Marx's method. However, whilst being ever mindful of the complexities involved, I shall argue that quite distinctive features of Marx's approach towards the study of economics can be identified. I cannot hope to present anything like an outline of Marx's vast range of writings in philosophy, politics, history and economics. Rather I shall focus upon the approach he adopted in the study of economics.

Karl Marx was born in Trier in 1818 of Jewish parents. He initially studied law at the University of Bonn but after a year decided to study philosophy at the University of Berlin, where he became involved with a radical group known as the Young Hegelians. At this time he intended pursuing an academic career in philosophy, but this ambition was frustrated and in turning away from academia, Marx began writing and editing a newspaper, the *Rheinische Zeitung*. This period proved particularly important in his intellectual development: he began to realise that writing on current affairs required a deep understanding of subjects such as economics, politics, philosophy and history and in his capacity as an editor he also experienced much state censorship which did much to push Marx further to the left in his political views. For a few years he lived in different countries, often incurring the displeasure of the authorities with his increasingly radical writings.

Eventually, Marx settled in London with his wife and children, until his death in 1883. His time in London was both a difficult and a creative part of his life. It was difficult because his financial resources were often meagre, however, freelance journalism, inheritances to his wife and the generous help of his friend and collaborator Friedrich Engels did much to ease their financial worries. This enabled Marx more time to concentrate on his *magnum opus, Das Kapital (Capital)*, which was regrettably uncompleted at the time of his death.

In what follows I shall consider some of the main methodological features of Marx's work and how these have been characterised. Then I shall consider some of the criticisms of this approach, especially those of Popper, and conclude with an assessment of Marx.

THE STARTING POINT

With Marx, a particularly difficult feature for any analysis is its starting point, that is, what are the categories and preconceptions that we can usefully begin with? This is related to a concern of his which was the distinction between 'appearances' (phenomena) and 'essence': appearances are not necessarily false, but they can mislead; essences refer to the basic organic relationships that underpin the phenomena that we are investigating. To Marx, if there was no difference between appearance and essence then there would be no need for science. He illustrated the difficulties of distinguishing the difference between essence and appearance when considering the study of the economy with the notion of population. At first sight this may appear 'real and concrete', but:

> Nevertheless this is shown, upon closer consideration, to be false. Population is an abstraction, if I omit the classes, for example, of which it consists. These classes are an empty word if I do not know the elements on which they are based. For example, wage-labour, capital etc. These imply exchange, division of labour, prices etc. Capital, for example, is nothing without wage-labour, without value, money, price etc. Therefore if I begin with population, then that would be a chaotic conception of the whole, and through closer determination I would come analytically to increasingly simpler concepts; from the conceptualized concrete to more and more tenuous abstractions, until I arrived at the simplest determinations. From there the journey would be taken up again in reverse until I finally arrived again at population, this time, however, not [with population] as a chaotic conception of a whole, but as a rich totality of many determinations and relationships. The first way [of proceeding] is one which political economy has taken up historically in its formation. The economists of the seventeenth century, for example, always began with the living whole, the population, the nation, the state, more states etc; they always end, however, in such a way that they discover a few determining, abstract, universal relationships, like division of labour, money, value etc., through analysis. As soon as these individual moments were more or less fixed and abstracted, the economic systems which ascend from the simple [moment], such as labour,

division of labour, need [and] exchange-value up to the state, exchange among nations and the world market, began [to be formulated]. The latter is obviously the scientifically correct method. (Marx, 1975, p. 72)

Marx is explaining the proper use of the 'power of abstraction'. What he is attempting to do is emphasise the importance of going beyond *empty* abstractions to the most simple and crucial relationships.

The above quotation also contains an allusion to another methodological concern of primary signficance to Marx – the method of analysis employed by some of the classical economists. Marx's attitude towards this group of economists was a mixture of, not uncritical, admiration, for David Ricardo and, to a lesser extent, Adam Smith and extreme distaste for the 'vulgar' economists such as Jean-Baptiste Say, Nassau Senior and Frédéric Bastiat. The 'vulgar' economists were so-called because they were regarded as being little more than apologists for the capitalist system. Indeed, Marx likened them to hired prize-fighters!

More generally, Marx classified most of his classical predecessors as 'bourgeois' economists. This was because they tended to study economics in an *a*historical and *a*social fashion and they generally assumed that the capitalist system was a universal system. For Marx, however, there had been, and would continue to be, different stages of social development and consequently, differing social relationships would have implications for our economic analysis. We could not pretend to conduct our analysis without some contemplation of historical and social considerations. Such an approach clearly meant that 'appearances' were very much more likely to receive attention than 'essences' and Marx illustrated this when he caricatured the classical approach (Marx, 1975, pp. 56–7). Here Marx portrayed classical economics in a way that anticipated the later marginal productivity theory of distribution. This conveys the impression of a well-ordered interaction between businessmen and workers which argues that these factors of production receive rewards equal to their respective marginal productivities, which gives an illusion of fairness. For Marx this superficial analysis did not consider the essentially exploitative relationship between capitalist and worker.

It is interesting that Marx viewed the orthodoxy of his day in this manner because the general approach is not too dissimilar from today's neo-classical orthodoxy. This should not be totally surprising because the economics of Say, Senior and Bastiat anticipated many of the important features of the marginalist revolution of the 1870s (see Dobb, 1977, ch. 4; and Hunt, 1979, ch. 6). The marginalist revolution in turn has been very influential in shaping today's orthodoxy and therefore Marx's criticisms of the classicals are likely to retain some relevance for contemporary economists. I shall consider this point later.

Marx also disliked the way in which the classical method emphasised the seemingly harmonious operation of the capitalist system as he felt that the social relationships of capitalist production were anything but harmonious. It is here that Marx employed the device of dialectics in order to aid him in his goal of bridging the gap between 'appearance' and 'essence'. The notion of the dialectic is associated with the German philosopher G. W. F. Hegel and as it is the most distinctive, and radical, feature of Marx's method it requires some consideration. Several writers (for example, Pilling, 1980; Rosdolsky, 1980; and Zelený, 1980) have made strong arguments for the detailed consideration of the linkage between Hegel and Marx. Indeed, they argue that if this crucial connection is not fully appreciated a vital part of Marx's approach will be misunderstood.

THE NOTION OF THE DIALECTIC

Hegel, writing in the early part of the nineteenth century, was also concerned with the difference between appearance and essence. He saw the world as an interconnected whole that was in endless motion. This was significant because Hegel was responding to what he saw as the overly mechanistic nature of science that had developed from the work of Descartes in particular and such developments had encouraged the increasing separation and specialisation of the different sciences. Hegel preferred a more organic approach and one implication of this is that a far more interdisciplinary methodology would result, something Marx embraced with relish.

To combat these mechanistic attitudes Hegel proposed the use of dialectics and he formulated three laws of dialectics. The first law concerned the transformation of quantity into quality, and vice versa; this law helps us to understand how new qualities develop out of seemingly insignificant quantitative changes – that is, a succession of quantitative changes initially do not affect the character of something until a certain point where it is transformed. An example of this is if the temperature of water is gradually reduced it will remain liquid. However, once its temperature falls below 0°C it turns into ice: that is, it becomes solid, but as the temperature rises the ice will melt and it will become water again.

The second law of dialectics refers to the unity of opposites. This emphasises the essentially contradictory nature of reality and for Hegel, movement stems from contradiction. The opposites that we observe in reality often form a coherent unity, that is, somehow what appears ephemeral is often one part of an ongoing process of which it forms an important part. Hegel (1966, pp. 70–1) utilised the example of an apple bud to illustrate what he meant:

> The bud disappears when the blossom breaks through, and we might say that the former is refuted by the latter, in the same way when the fruit comes, the blossom may be explained to be a false form of the plant's existence, for the fruit appears as its true nature in the place of the blossom . . . .

He continues:

> These stages are not merely differentiated; they supplant one another. But the ceaseless activity of their own inherent nature makes them at the same time moments of an organic unity where one is as necessary as the other; and this equal necessity of all moments constitutes alone and thereby the life of the whole.

The unity of this second law of dialectics is best viewed as something relative: it refers to a temporary position only. What is more interesting to dialecticians is the search for the change and motion arising from the inherent contradictions.

The third law of dialectics is the negation of the negation. This is more usually referred to as thesis, antithesis and synthesis. Here the original theory (the thesis) is replaced by an opposite, contradictory theory (the antithesis) and this in turn is superseded by a more sophisticated theory which incorporates aspects of both thesis and antithesis (the synthesis).

This approach clearly has significant implications for the way in which we study phenomena. For Hegel, 'truth is the whole', that is, we need to comprehend reality by studying the contradictory and organic processes in their totality and implicit within this approach is a rejection of the kind of naïve inductivism and instrumentalism discussed earlier. Piecemeal inductive facts of experience are likely to mislead us into accepting surface phenomena. Indeed, one of the key objects of much empirical analysis is to seek regularities and order, but such analyses will not necessarily convey the contradictory character of relationships desired by a dialectician.

Marx found Hegel's notion of the dialectic very useful, but he objected to Hegel's more idealistic way of employing the principle (Marx, 1976, p. 102). He favoured a more 'materialist' interpretation of the dialectic – this means that 'the material world' is 'reflected in the mind of man, and translated into forms of thought'.

Marx saw much potential for his more materialist conception of the dialectic. To begin with his criticism of the orthodox economists received most ammunition – by focusing upon contradictions as a dynamic method, the orthodox approach, which emphasised harmony and was static, was bound to be unsatisfactory. Following on the caricature of the orthodox method referred to above, Marx gave us a flavour of a more dialectical way of thinking. He objected to the way in which the 'bourgeois' economists separated different economic categories, such as production and consumption, as if they were discrete. Rather, we should view things in the following manner:

> Therefore production is immediately consumption, [and] consumption is immediately production. Each is immediately its opposite. At the same time, however, a mediating movement takes place between the two. Production mediates consumption, whose material it creates; without production, consumption lacks an object. However, consumption also mediates production, since it creates first the subject for the products, the subject for which they are products. The product only receives its last finish in consumption. A railway on which no one rides, which is therefore not worn out, which is not consumed, is only a railway virtually, not a railway in actuality. Without production there is no consumption; however, without consumption there is no production, since production [without consumption] would be purposeless. (Marx, 1975, pp. 59–60)

Prior to this passage Marx castigates the 'bourgeois' economists for their undialectical way of thinking which led them into the false separation of such categories. The notion of the dialectic also indicates why Marx was so unhappy with the *a*historical nature of much of 'bourgeois' economic analysis. His three volume *Theories of Surplus Value* was a criticial survey of the theories of value of economists that preceded him. However, this work is not a straightforward history of economic thought in the sense in which we usually understand it. For Marx, we needed to study not only the history of societies, but of the ideas within them. This was because such ideas were often a reflection of the state of development of that society and were clearly an important part of it and this applied to the work of economists. The mercantilists reflected the situation of merchant capitalism, the classicals the development of industrial capitalism and by subjecting their theories to critical scrutiny Marx was discovering not only the contradictions of Ricardo, Say and Bastiat, but also some of the wider contradictions of an emerging capitalist economy.

By the time Marx came to write *Capital* he recognised that the dialectic had never before been employed by economists. How did it shape the development of that massive work? I cannot hope to provide anything like a summary of a work that runs to more than two thousand pages; instead, I shall consider, in broad terms, some of the contradictory forces that Marx identified as motivating the development, and likely demise, of the capitalist system.

Volumes 1 and 2 of *Capital* are best regarded as preliminary stages in which a multitude of relationships and facets of the capitalist system are considered. These considerations are brought together in Volume 3 where something approaching a consideration of the 'totality' of capitalism is undertaken.

Volume 1 is possibly, especially the opening chapter, the most obviously dialectical of Marx's analyses within *Capital*. Recalling the importance that he attributed to the starting point of our analysis, Marx selects the 'cell-form' of the capitalist system – the commodity. At this stage Marx was not concerned with viewing commodities and their relationship to prices, money, and so on. His method of abstraction forced him to extract the most fundamental features of capitalism and prices and money were very much surface phenomena that required investigation at a much later stage of his analysis.

The most crucial feature of Marx's analysis, from a dialectical point of view, is his consideration of the commodity 'labour power'. By considering this the vital relationship between capitalist and wage labourer is closely scrutinised. Marx considers the socially necessary amount of labour power that each labourer needs to expend in order to live and rear children, that is, to reproduce his own labour power. If the necessities of food, shelter and clothing (which were not regarded as a bare subsistence level by Marx,) required only five hours' work a day this would be the socially necessary amount of labour time. However, if those workers were employed for fifteen hours a day, then the other ten hours would be solely for the benefit of their capitalist employer. From this it was a short step for Marx to derive the important notion of surplus value and, from this, profits. Capitalists are generally assumed by Marx to seek to accumulate increased profits and improve their productive capacities and consequently there is the situation of a real conflict between the interests of the capitalist and the worker. Volume 1 is replete with empirical detail relating to the struggle over the length of the working day – given Marx's analysis, capitalists would appropriate more surplus value, and ultimately more profits, if the length of the working day were extended and/or wages were reduced. Therefore we have an explanation of how the seeds of class struggle are sown.

Volume 2 introduces the important notions of differing forms of capital. Constant capital refers to tools, machines, buildings and raw materials, that is, non-human means of capital. Marx referred to such items as constant capital because they did not confer, by themselves, any surplus value upon the final product, as was the case with variable capital which relates to labour power. Organic capital was defined as the ratio of constant to variable capital and from this Marx considers how there is a tendency for the organic composition of capital to increase. This implies a rapid increase in technological advance and with it an increase in the size of productive units and ultimately the concentration of industry. Volume 2 also raises the possibility of periodic crises within the capitalist economy and there are real tensions here: if the conditions of the workers are not improved, where will the markets for the ever-increasing production of goods be? The likelihood is that gluts, and periodic crises, will result and the conditions of the workers will become more desperate as unemployment increases.

By Volume 3 these tensions are brought together to consider capitalism as more of a totality, but Marx never fulfilled this task – he died before he could incorporate other volumes of *Capital* dealing with international trade, money and world crises. However, a more complete picture begins to emerge in Volume 3. It is here that Marx examines his famous law of the tendency of the rate of profit to fall in a capitalist economy, although this is heavily qualified. The point is that the endogenously-generated conflicts and contradictions that are the very nature of the capitalist system will lead to its ultimate negation and replacement by another, opposite, form of society – socialism.

This classic dialectical scenario was precisely what Marx anticipated and he realised that it was this very emphasis upon dialectics that made his analysis so unpalatable to 'bourgeois' economists and capitalists alike. Of the dialectic he wrote:

In its rational form it is a scandal and an abomination to the bourgeoisie and its doctrinaire spokesmen, because it includes in its positive understanding of what exists a simultaneous recognition of its negation, its inevitable destruction; because it regards every historically developed form as being in a fluid state, in motion, and therefore grasps its transient aspect as well; and because it does not let itself be impressed by anything, being in its very essence critical and revolutionary.

The fact that the movement of capitalist society is full of contradictions impresses itself most strikingly on the practical bourgeois in the changes of the periodic cycle through which modern industry passes, the summit of which is the general crisis. (Marx, 1976, p. 103)

The notion of the dialectic also holds important implications for the way in which Marx viewed the concept of causality. We are no longer dealing with a purely mechanical notion of causality, one which moves in one direction only. By adopting a dialectical approach we are committed to analysing the economy as an organism, a totality. Here causal connections are not predominantly one-way, at any point in time – although such relationships exist in *Capital* – but are simultaneous and reciprocal. We are now inhabiting a world of action, reaction and interaction and Marx cites several examples of this, such as, 'The greatness of the Romans was the cause of their conquests, and their conquests destroyed their greatness. Wealth is the cause of luxury and luxury has a destructive effect on wealth' (Marx, 1981, p. 552). Numerous similar examples are to be found in Marx's writings. Some of the implications of this will be considered shortly.

CATEGORISING MARX

Is it possible to categorise Marx's method neatly? I doubt it. However, this has not discouraged many from making the effort. It should be clear by now that Marx would have had little time for the inductivism outlined in Chapter 1: the crucial distinction between appearance and essence alone is suggestive of this. Indeed, one of Pilling's (1980) strongest arguments against much contemporary Marxist and anti-Marxist analysis is that it tries to accommodate Marx's work within a narrow empiricist framework. Pilling refers to the example of the post-1945 boom in the UK economy and the success of Keynesian interventionism during that period. At the time this signalled to many the end of the business cycle and severe capitalist crises. Consequently, it was felt that a central feature of Marx's analysis was no longer relevant. However, Pilling argues against such claims in the following terms:

For if we wish to form an adequate conception of this period we must get to the *essence* of this boom, to its real contradictory nature. And this we cannot do simply by 'reading off' a series of surface phenomena (indices of production, of living standards, etc). (Pilling, 1980, p. 30)

Instead, Marx's analysis needs to be judged more against the development of the underlying contradictions within the economy during this century. This is because the twentieth century marks the era of a more developed form of capitalism than that analysed by Marx – monopoly capitalism – and Pilling is correct in this.

Marx felt uneasy about deriving things inductively because this often implied an uncritical acceptance of the interpretations of the particular facts upon which the inductive generalisation is based. A point that requires clarification here is the distinction between 'empirical' and 'empiricist'. To be empirical in approach means that one endeavours to go to some lengths to substantiate, or refute, one's theories by considering factual or other data and Marx certainly engaged in this activity. He was an avid reader of the government 'blue books' published last century providing statistics of output and employment in different industries. Indeed, in order to obtain some information from an untranslated Russian source he learnt the language. However, to be an empiricist is something quite different. Here we embrace a whole approach towards the acquisition of knowledge that can only be obtained through sensory perception and facts, and through independent testing and so on, an approach very similar to inductivism and instrumentalism, but Marx did not accept this programme. As Pilling notes, he was critical of empiricism because it encouraged a concentration on the *source* of knowledge, rather than its *form*. Sayer (1983) makes many similar arguments and suggests also that Marx rejected *a priorism*, that is, extreme deductivism.

Despite these points there are those who still maintain that Marx was essentially an empiricist (Hudelson, 1982) and even a positivist, but both of these claims should be questionable on the basis of what I have stated above and they are both decisively, and convincingly, repudiated by Farr (1983 and 1984).

CRITICISM OF MARX

Rather than attempt to categorise Marx's method, it seems more appropriate to regard it as a very distinctive approach that should be considered on its own merits, so what are these? Many have made critical observations of Marx's method and the most notable critique has been Popper's, who particularly dislikes the notion of the dialectic.

The very nature of the dialectic is too 'loose' and 'metaphysical' (Popper, 1972, p. 322). Popper makes a valid point here: he feels that the dialectic can be so wide ranging that it entails 'everything but yet nothing' and this can arise due to the complex notion of causality associated with the dialectic. This point is also brought out in Wedberg (1982, pp. 188–9). He cites Engels' conception of dialectical causality, which seems to have received Marx's blessing: Engels refers to the situation where the feedback effects render an event a cause at one moment and an effect in another and there can be very serious problems here for testability. Dialectics are very exciting and all-embracing, but they can easily be too 'vague' and 'loose', as Popper claims and it can clearly be notoriously difficult to pin down causal connections for testing purposes: one can simply argue that a situation was too complex or not right to obtain clear-cut results. Howard and King (1985, p. 31) note that this can leave a dialectical perspective 'not directly amenable to empirical testing', and being 'consequently largely immune from criticism on factual grounds'. Not surprisingly, Popper has scented the unpleasant aroma of unfalsifiability. The dialectic, as we have seen, is not so much an empiricist phenomenon, but is an important factor in our understanding of the empirical. Is Marx's work unfalsifiable? It is difficult to test. However, given the problems of the Duhem–Quine thesis, this is a difficulty not unique to Marx; it haunts most forms of theoretical analysis that we desire to test. Mandel (1976, p. 24; and 1983) has argued that Popper is wrong to argue that *Capital* is untestable. He points out that many of the logical implications and conditional predictions are susceptible to tests and many have been verified. For example, Marx predicted the increasing concentration of industry in fewer and much larger hands, and that periodic crises would become more severe (witness the 1890s, 1920s, 1930s, and now 1980s). Also Mandel has endeavoured to consider the contemporary relevance of Marx's analysis and finds it in good shape.

Popper (1976b) also argued that Marx was guilty of 'historicism'. This essentially relates to Marx's 'commitment' to the view that there exists an inexorable law of historical development that will necessarily result in the ultimate triumph of socialism. According to Popper, Marx's 'uncritical' acceptance of contradictions when employing dialectical reasoning prevented him from searching for ways to alleviate such contradictions and this in turn led Marx to adopt 'economic determinism'. This is where economic forces predominantly influence the development of society. For Popper, human behaviour is essentially individual in nature (recall his methodological individualism) and therefore can, and sometimes should, change the course of history.

Is this charge of 'economic determinism' valid? Marx did leave himself open to misinterpretation here – and he gleefully signalled 'the death knell of capitalism where the expropriator would be expropriated'. However, as Sherman (1981) indicates, too much can be made of this. He cites another passage from Marx where he states that men do make their own history, but not under the conditions of their choosing. They are likely to be constrained by the institutional and social structures that they have inherited. Sayer (1983) points out that the triumph of socialism, as opposed to the demise of capitalism, was a prognosis, a piece of wishful thinking, rather than a prediction logically derived from his theory.

Indeed, Marx was careful to qualify some of his analyses that related to the collapse of capitalism and this applied most notably to his consideration of the tendency of the rate of profit to fall. Here he argued that there were liable to be several counteracting forces. Such forces could also stave off the decline of capitalism. For example, depressing wages and increasing the length of the working day would help to offset the decline in the rate of profit. Also reducing the cost of constant capital, such as machinery and raw materials, would do the same. Presumably technological advances would be important here. The other key factor was to sell more goods in foreign markets and here a rapid expansion of overseas markets could be particularly significant, but Marx did not live long enough to develop this point. However, the implications for a more developed form of capitalism – imperialism – were there to be developed.

It seems that Popper's general criticisms are not very accurate, a point that Hudelson (1980) makes. He also argues that Popper appears to accept implicitly that Marx's economic analysis is not meaningless pseudo-science and that some testable predictions, as we have seen above, can be obtained from it.

These types of criticisms, coupled with the problems of easily categorising Marx's method, have led Marxist writers to adopt different positions. As I have noted above, writers such as Pilling, Rosdolsky and Zelený regard dialectics as one of the most distinctive features of Marxism. However as Gorman (1981) demonstrates, in a very interesting article, there has been a strand of empirical Marxism opposed to this view. Gorman considers the work of Eduard Bernstein, Galvano Della Volpe and Lucio Colletti, the latter being one of the strongest critics of dialectics: he sees it as being metaphysical and superficial, and something which gives Marxism a bad name.

More recently, Elster (1985) has reinterpreted Marx's methodology in far more radical terms. He clearly sees Marx's Hegelian lineage as being of 'little or no intrinsic interest', indeed he views the use of dialectics as a 'disastrous scientific practice'. This in itself is not new, but what is different about Elster's treatment is the way in which he seeks to recast Marx's method. He sees no inconsistency in claiming that Marx was a 'pioneer' in utilising methodological individualism. We saw in the last chapter how methodological individualists usually saw their methodology as being opposed to Marxist methodology.

Whilst I find many of Elster's criticisms of Marx perceptive and valid I feel uneasy about his characterisation. It seems to me inconceivable, as Elster appears to suggest, that Marx could be interpreted as adopting a methodology that somehow resembles the methodological individualism and static equilibrium analysis of neo-classical economics.

Whatever the weaknesses and limitations of dialectics I consider Marx's very distinctive approach to be a real alternative to the sterility of much orthodox method currently undertaken. I noted earlier that Marx was attacking the orthodoxy of his day. However, in many important respects the current situation is very similar. Marx found mathematical analysis very useful in his own work, but it is unlikely that he would appreciate the lengths to which contemporary economists have taken such analysis. Mathematical techniques such as Lagrange Multipliers and econometric techniques, for example regression analysis, are frequently *a*historical and *a*social. Indeed, many econometricians unwittingly recognise the importance of the dialectical notion of causality. For several years they have been making big strides in developing simultaneous equation estimation, such as two- and three-stage least squares analysis, partly in response to the acknowledged need to take more account of feedback and reciprocity in econometric equations.

Also the more holistic, dynamic and interdisciplinary approach which was favoured by Marx is beginning to receive more attention amongst economists. To be sure there are problems in trying to adopt such a method, however there is a real sense in which our current techniques are too easy and mechanical and this discourages us from being adventurous when bold steps are necessary. I believe that methodologically Marx pointed us in a direction that is worth following. Indeed, as Howard and King (1985, p. 239) argue, Marx's method remains the most 'pertinent' aspect of his political economy.

Conclusion

In this concluding section I will consider some possible directions that future methodological discussions could take. I have argued elsewhere (Pheby, 1986) that considerations of economic methodology have been too strongly influenced by the natural sciences. What is required is the development of our own distinct methodologies. We have seen above the long history of 'naturalism' within economics, but very few economists have bothered to evaluate critically whether this has benefited economics. There seems to be an implicit belief that if only we can imitate the natural sciences then their success will somehow rub off on to economics.

However, those who have taken the trouble to challenge this view have some important things to say and the most eloquent and perceptive has been G. L. S. Shackle (1972). For Shackle, the 'impossibility of prediction' in economics is a necessary implication of the fact that economic change is linked to changes in knowledge which we cannot know before they have occurred. He calls this the 'human predicament'. Furthermore, once we acknowledge the existence of time we are forced to consider expectations, uncertainty and ignorance. Shackle has perceptively recognised the way in which economists have utilised the Cartesian method in order to deal with such problems and he believes that the resulting heavy emphasis upon the role of reason has had undesirable consequences. By placing a premium on abstraction and simplification, a rather mechanistic and deterministic type of economics has evolved. Shackle is not opposed to abstraction as such, indeed it forms an essential part of our intellectual armoury. What he does object to is abstraction that assumes away important aspects of economic reality such as uncertainty and expectations. He also feels that this emphasis upon reason offers us some form of safety and security against such awkward considerations. However, it is a misleading security.

Shackle has also criticised the empirical side of economics which has developed its own ways of coping with the 'human predicament'. This applies particularly to the widespread use of the frequency theory of probability. The frequency approach necessarily relies upon a large number of observations or trials in order to assign numerical probabilities. Shackle argues that for many important decisions within economics such extensive information is not available and this applies particularly to one-off situations. For example, entrepreneurs do not make major investment decisions very frequently and in conseqence an important type of economic decision will receive little assistance from the frequency approach in overcoming the difficulties posed by uncertainty and expectations.

Another point which distinguishes economics from the natural sciences is pertinent to Shackle's considerations. When tossing coins or throwing dice the nature of the environment is stable, but a major investment decision will itself often materially affect the environment, that is, the industry, in which it is made. The unknown consequences of such a course of action are vitally important, especially in an oligopolistic situation.

Similar arguments have been made by Fritjof Capra. He questions the widespread imitation, by the social sciences, of the natural sciences:

> However, the Cartesian framework is often quite inappropriate for the phenomena they are describing, and consequently their models have become increasingly unrealistic. This is now especially apparent in economics. Present-day economics is characterised by the fragmentary and reductionist approach that typifies most social sciences. Economists generally fail to recognise that the economy is merely one aspect of a whole ecological and social fabric; a living system composed of human beings in continual interaction with one another and with their natural resources, most of which are, in turn, living organisms. The basic error of the social sciences is to divide this fabric into fragments, assumed to be independent and to be dealt with in separate academic departments. (Capra, 1983, pp. 194–5)

Another problem of adopting a mechanistic approach within economics is the need to assume, and work within, a stable institutional environment. Neo-classical orthodoxy is regarded as being, more or less, appropriate to the institutions that existed in the late Victorian period. However, in the late twentieth century the industrial scene is dominated by multinationals and oligopolies and these do not conform to the convenient fiction of perfect competition. Furthermore, much orthodox economics relies heavily upon static equilibrium analysis. In this world of political, social and economic upheaval, such analyses too easily become sterile exercises in avoiding consideration of such vital factors.

The last point I wish to make about naturalism within economics is to query its appropriateness on its own terms. I have indicated above a number of limitations of such methodologies that, at the very least, force us to think carefully about adopting them unthinkingly. However, in his challenging book, Capra argues that much of the older mechanistic methodologies have been largely superseded within the natural sciences. He indicates how a more organic and less deterministic approach has been adopted in many areas with no great loss to their succcess or effectiveness and this is an interesting point because few economic methodologists employ illustrative examples from the recent history of the natural sciences. Instead, we are provided with remote examples such as Copernican astronomy and Newtonian physics, but because of their largely inappropriate nature I have deliberately refrained from using such examples in this book. Therefore, if economists wish to continue to emulate the natural sciences it seems that we need to review our methodologies.

How can this be done? Capra provides us with some guidance:

> I believe that the most useful approach would be not to abandon economics as such, but to regard the framework of current economic thought, so deeply rooted in the Cartesian paradigm, as a scientific model that has become outdated. It may well continue to be useful for limited microeconomic analyses, but will certainly need to be modified and expanded. The new theory, or set of models, is likely to involve a systems approach that will integrate biology, psychology, political philosophy and several branches of human knowledge together with economics into a broad ecological framework . . . Their approach is still scientific, but goes beyond the Cartesian–Newtonian image of science. The empirical basis includes not only ecological data, social and political facts and psychological phenomena, but also a clear reference to cultural values. From this basis such scientists will be able to build realistic and reliable models of economic phenomena. (Capra, 1983, p. 247)

Capra recognises that we will not be able to completely abandon economics as we know it today and there are two main reasons for this. Firstly, the institutional structure of academic economics is still heavily committed to traditional methods and approaches. Those skilled in mathematics and econometrics have a vested interest in maintaining the *status quo*. Secondly, we do not need to completely reject orthodox techniques: statistical and mathematical analyses form a valuable part of our work. The problem that has arisen is that these techniques are often pursued as ends in themselves, as support for the view that the more we employ them the more scientific economics becomes. The central implication of Capra's programme is that we become significantly less dependent upon such techniques.

Some of the methodologies discussed above have a role to play in this and I see the work of Laudan as being particularly valuable. He has provided us with the basis for a useful structural theory that will enable us to employ meaningful, but flexible, standards in assessing our work. Methodological standards are something which it is easy to be sanctimonious about; however, it would be foolish to deny that we require some reference to them – this is, in fact, one of the main reasons why we study methodology. And it is important for us to employ this structured methodology in a way that will enable us to assess how well we have performed.

Whilst Laudan can provide us with a flexible and general method of appraisal, something extra is required and it is here that the work of the Austrians and Marx is pertinent. The Austrians' emphasis upon subjectivism, time, uncertainty and expectations is a necessary component for a different type of economics that wishes to comprehend the complexities of the modern world. Indeed, as noted earlier, the Austrians' willingness to adopt limited statistical work and engage in interdisciplinary activities are promising signs for the future.

Marx, despite some uncertainty as to the adequacy of his dialectics, has much to offer. He provided us with evidence of how rich an analysis incorporating an organic, interdisciplinary approach can be. However, there is one important element still lacking. This is a convincing theory of institutions and their change. The work of a group of economists known as the Institutionalists could prove valuable here: the contribution of writers such as Thorstein Veblen, J. R. Commons and J. K. Galbraith warrants close attention.

These considerations help to bring out the dangers of adopting an excessively paradigmatic attitude when examining seemingly alternative paradigms. This could easily lead us to regard Austrians, Marxists and Institutionalists as having little grounds for cohabitation, but this would be a ludicrously blinkered view. It is precisely this type of narrow-mindedness that will continue to hold economics back and I firmly believe that we can learn from greater cross-fertilisation between 'different' paradigms. I am heartened by growing evidence of this happening: for example, Eichner (1985) has developed an approach incorporating the work of the Institutionalists and Post-Keynesians; Hodgson (1987) is integrating aspects of Institutionalism, Austrianism and Post-Keynesianism; and the stimulating work of Earl (1983 and 1984) is employing psychology in order to develop an alternative theory of consumer and business behaviour. Earl also draws upon the work of the Austrians, Post-Keynesians and Institutionalists. These are exciting developments, but there still needs to be a far greater emphasis upon more interdisciplinary co-operation.

This will not be an easy programme to work on and it will require much more widely read and flexible economists: a heavy and easy reliance upon a handful of formal techniques will simply not be adequate. The way ahead is not easy, but it is challenging and stimulating and I believe that it is the way towards a more dynamic, less cloistered type of economics that future generations may come to thank us for adopting.

Bibliography

AGASSI, J. (1969) 'The Novelty of Popper's Philosophy of Science', *International Philosophical Quarterly*, vol. 8, pp. 442–63.

AGASSI, J. (1979) 'The Legacy of Lakatos', *Philosophy of the Social Sciences*, vol. 9, pp. 316–26.

ARCHIBALD, G. C. (1979) 'Method and Appraisal in Economics', *Philosophy of the Social Sciences*, vol. 9, pp. 304–15.

BAUMBERGER, J. (1977) 'No Kuhnian Revolutions in Economics', *Journal of Economic Issues*, vol. 11, March, pp. 1–20.

BLACK, F. (1982) 'The Trouble with Econometric Models', *Financial Analyst Journal*, vol. 35, March/April, pp. 29–37.

BLAUG, M. (1976) 'Kuhn versus Lakatos or Paradigms versus Research Programmes in the History of Economics', pp. 149–80 from S. J. Latsis (ed.), *Method and Appraisal in Economics* (Cambridge: Cambridge University Press).

BLAUG, M. (1980) *The Methodology of Economics: or How Economists Explain*, (London: Cambridge University Press).

BLOCK, W. (1973) 'A Comment on "The Extraordinary Claim of Praxeology", by Professor Gutiérrez', *Theory and Decision*, vol. 3, pp. 377–87.

BÖHM, S. (1985) Letter to J. Pheby, 12 October 1985.

BOLAND, L. A. (1979) 'A Critique of Friedman's Critics', *Journal of Economic Literature*, vol. 17, June, pp. 503–22.

BOLAND, L. A. (1982) *The Foundations of Economic Method* (London: George Allen & Unwin).

BRONFENBRENNER, M. (1971) 'The "Structure of Revolutions" in Economic Thought', *History of Political Economy*, vol. 3, no. 1, pp. 136–51.

CAIRNES, J. E. (1875) *The Character and Logical Method of Political Economy*, 2nd edn (London: Macmillan).

CALDWELL, B. J. (1980) 'A Critique of Friedman's Methodological Instrumentalism', *Southern Economic Journal*, vol. 47, October, pp. 366–74.

CALDWELL, B. J. (1982) *Beyond Positivism: Economic Methodology in the Twentieth Century* (London: George Allen & Unwin).

CALDWELL, B. J. (1984) 'Praxeology and its Critics: an Appraisal', *History of Political Economy*, vol. 16, Fall, pp. 363–79.

CALDWELL, B. J. (1985) 'Disentangling Hayek, Hutchison and Popper on the Methodology of Economics', mimeo.

CANTERBURY, E. R. and BURKHARDT, R. J. (1983) 'What do we mean by asking whether Economics is a Science?' in A. S. Eichner (ed.) (1983), *Why Economics is not yet a Science* (London: Macmillan).

CAPRA, F. (1983) *The Turning Point* (London: Fontana).

CHALMERS, A. F. (1982) *What is this thing called Science?* 2nd edn (Milton Keynes: Open University Press).

COATS, A. W. (1954) 'The Historicist Reaction in English Political Economy, 1870–90', *Economica*, vol. 21, May, pp. 143–53.

CODDINGTON, A. (1972) 'Positive Economics', *Canadian Journal of Economics*, vol. 5, pp. 1–15.

COPI, M. (1978) *Introduction to Logic*, 5th edn (New York: Collier–Macmillan).

CROSS, R. (1982) 'The Duhem–Quine Thesis, Lakatos and the Appraisal of Theories in Macroeconomics', *Economic Journal*, vol. 92, June, pp. 320–40.

CROSS, R. (1984) 'Monetarism and Duhem's Thesis', in P. Wiles and G. Routh (eds) *Economics in Disarray* (Oxford: Basil Blackwell).

DAVIDSON, P. (1978) 'Post Keynesian Economics', in D. Bell and I. Kristol (eds), *The Crisis in Economic Theory* (New York: Basic Books).

DOBB, M. (1977) *Theories of Value and Distribution Since Adam Smith: Ideology and Economic Theory* (Cambridge: Cambridge University Press).

DOPPELT, G. (1981) 'Larry Laudan's Pragmatic Alternative', *Inquiry*, vol. 42, part 2, pp. 253–71.

DOW, S. (1985) *Macroeconomic Thought: A Methodological Approach* (Oxford: Basil Blackwell).

EARL, P. E. (1983) *The Economic Imagination* (Brighton: Wheatsheaf).

EARL, P. E. (1984) *The Corporate Imagination* (Brighton: Wheatsheaf).

EICHNER, A. S. (1983) (ed.), *Why Economics is Not Yet a Science* (London: Macmillan).

EICHNER, A. S. (1985) *Toward a New Economics* (London: Macmillan).

ELSTER, J. (1985) *Making Sense of Marx* (Cambridge: Cambridge University Press).

FARR, J. (1983) 'Marx No Empiricist', *Philosophy of the Social Sciences*, vol. 13, pp. 464–72.

FARR, J. (1984) 'Marx and Positivism', in T. Ball and J. Farr (eds) *After Marx* (Cambridge: Cambridge University Press).

FEYERABEND, P. (1978) *Against Method: Outline of an Anarchistic Theory of Knowledge* (London: Verso).

FEYERABEND, P. (1981) 'More Clothes from the Emperor's Bargain Basement', *British Journal for the Philosophy of Science*, vol. 32, pp. 57–94.

FRIEDMAN, M. (1953) 'The Methodology of Positive Economics', in *Essays in Positive Economics* (Chicago: Chicago University Press).

FRIEDMAN, M. (1970) *The Counter-Revolution in Monetary Theory*, IEA Occasional Paper, no. 33.

FULTON, G. (1984) 'Research Programmes in Economics', *History of Political Economy*, vol. 16, no. 2, pp. 187–206.

GOLDSTEIN, L. J. (1951) 'The Inadequacy of the Principle of Methodological Individualism', *The Journal of Philosophy*, vol. 53, pp. 801–13.

GORDON, R. A. (1965) 'The Contribution of the History of Economic Thought to the Understanding of Economic Theory, Economic History, and the History of Economic Policy', *American Economic Review*, vol. 55, pp. 119–27.

GORMAN, R. A. (1981) 'Empirical Marxism', in *History and Theory: Studies in the Philosophy of History*, no. 20, Wesleyan University Press.

GRAHL, J. (1977) 'Econometric Methods in Macroeconomics: A Critical Assessment', *British Review of Economic Issues*, vol. 1, no. 1, November, pp. 11–37.

GREEN, H. A. J. (1976) *Consumer Theory*, revised edn (London: Macmillan).

GUTIÉRREZ, C. (1971) 'The Extraordinary Claim of Praxeology', *Theory and Decision*, vol. 1, pp. 327–76.

HALL, R. L. and HITCH, C. J. (1939) 'Price Theory and Business Behaviour', *Oxford Economic Papers*, no. 2, May, pp. 12–45.

HANDS, D. W. (1979) 'The Methodology of Economic Research Programmes', *Philosophy of the Social Sciences*, vol. 9, pp. 293–303.

HANDS, D. W. (1984) 'Blaug's Economic Methodology', *Philosophy of the Social Sciences*, vol. 14, pp. 115–25.

HARWOOD, E. C. (1955) 'Human Action: A Treatise on Economics', in Harwood E. C. (ed.), *Reconstruction of Economics* (Great Barrington, Massachussetts: American Institute for Economic Research).

HAYEK, F. A. (1967) *Studies in Philosophy, Politics and Economics* (London: Routledge & Kegan Paul).

HAYEK, F. A. (1978) *New Studies in Philosophy, Politics, Economics and the History of Ideas* (London: Routledge & Kegan Paul).

HAYEK, F. A. (1979) *The Counter-Revolution of Science*, 2nd edn, (Indianapolis: Liberty Press).

HAYEK, F. A. (1980) *Individualism and Economic Order*, midway reprint (Chicago, Ill.: University of Chicago Press).

HEGEL, G. W. F. (1966) *The Phenomenology of Mind* (London: George Allen & Unwin).

HELM, D. (1984) 'Predictions and Causes: A Comparison of Friedman and Hicks on Method', *Oxford Economic Papers*, vol. 36, supplement, pp. 118–34.

HEMPEL, C. G. (1966) *Philosophy of Natural Science* (Englewood Cliffs, N. J.: Prentice-Hall).

HENDRY, D. F. (1980) 'Econometrics: Alchemy or Science?' *Economica*, vol. 47, pp. 387–406.

HESSE, M. (1967) 'Instrumentalism', in Edwards P. (ed.), *The Encyclopaedia of Philosophy* (London: Macmillan).

HINDESS, B. (1977) *Philosophy and Methodology in the Social Sciences* (Brighton: Harvester Press).

HODGSON, G. (1987) *Economics and Institutions* (Cambridge: Polity Press).

HOLLANDER, S. (1983) 'William Whewell and John Stuart Mill on the Methodology of Political Economy', *Studies in the History of Philosophy of Science*, vol. 14, no. 2, pp. 127–68.

HOWARD, M. C. and KING, J. E. (1985) *The Political Economy of Marx*, 2nd edn (London: Longmans).

HUDELSON, R. (1980) 'Popper's Critique of Marx', *Philosophical Studies*, vol. 37, pp. 258–71.

HUDELSON, R. (1982) 'Marx's Empiricism', *Philosophy of the Social Sciences* vol. 12, pp. 241–53.

HUME, D. (1975) *Enquiries concerning Human Understanding and concerning the Principles of Morals*, 3rd edn of L. A. Selby-Bigge version (Oxford: Oxford University Press).

HUNT, E. K. (1979) *History of Economic Thought: A Critical Perspective* (Belmont, Calif.: Wadsworth).

HUTCHISON, T. W. (1960) *The Significance and Basic Postulates of Economic Theory* (New York: Augustus Kelley).

HUTCHISON, T. W. (1976) 'On the History of Philosophy of Science and Economics' in S. J. Latsis (ed.), *Method and Appraisal in Economics* (Cambridge: Cambridge University Press).

HUTCHISON, T. W. (1981) *The Politics and Philosophy of Economics* (Oxford, Basil Blackwell).

HUTCHISON, T. W. (1984) 'Our Methodological Crisis', in P. Wiles and G. Routh (eds), *Economics in Disarray* (Oxford: Basil Blackwell).

JOHANSSON, I. (1975) *A Critique of Karl Popper's Methodology* (Stockholm: Scandinavian University Books).

JOHNSON, L. E. (1983) 'Economic Paradigms: A Missing Dimension', *Journal of Economic Issues*, vol. 17, December, pp. 1097-111.

KIRZNER, I. (1976) *The Economic Point of View*, 2nd edn (Kansas City: Sheed and Ward).

KLANT, J. J. (1984) *The Rules of the Game: The Logical Structure of Economic Theories* (Cambridge: Cambridge University Press).

KOOT, G. M. (1975) 'T. E. Cliffe Leslie, Irish Social Reform, and the Origins of the English Historical School of Economics', *History of Political Economy*, vol. 7, no. 3, pp. 312-36.

KOOT, G. M. (1980) 'English Historical Economics and the Emergence of Economic History in England', *History of Political Economy*, vol. 12, no. 2, pp. 174-205.

KOUTSOYIANNIS, A. (1979) *Modern Microeconomics*, 2nd edn (London: Macmillan).

KRIPS, H. (1980) 'Some Problems for "Progress and its Problems"', *Philosophy of Science*, vol. 47, pp. 601-16.

KUHN, T. S. (1970a) *The Structure of Scientific Revolutions*. Enlarged 2nd edn (Chicago, Ill.: University of Chicago Press).

KUHN, T. S. (1970b) 'Reflections on my Critics' in I. Lakatos and A. Musgrave (eds), *Criticism and the Growth of Knowledge* (Cambridge: Cambridge University Press).

KUHN, T. S. (1977) *The Essential Tension: Selected Studies in Scientific Tradition and Change* (Chicago: University of Chicago Press).

KUNIN, L. and WEAVER, F. S. (1971) 'On the Structure of Scientific Revolutions in Economics', *History of Political Economy*, vol. 3, no. 2, pp. 391-7.

LACHMANN, L. (1970) *The Legacy of Max Weber* (London: Heinemann Educational Books).

LACHMANN, L. (1977) *Capital, Expectations and the Market Process* (Kansas City: Sheed Andrews and McMeel).

LACHMANN, L. (1982) 'Ludwig von Mises and the Extension of Subjectivism' in I. Kirzner (ed.), *Method, Process and Austrian Economics: Essays in Honour of Ludwig von Mises* (Lexington, Mass.: D. C. Heath).

LAKATOS, I. (1970) 'Falsification and the Methodology of Scientific Research Programmes' in I. Lakatos and A. Musgrave (eds), *Criticism and the Growth of Knowledge* (Cambridge: Cambridge University Press).

LAKATOS, I. (1978) *The Methodology of Scientific Research Programmes* (Cambridge: Cambridge University Press).

LATSIS, S. J. (1976) 'A Research Programme in Economics' in S. J. Latsis (ed.) *Method and Appraisal in Economics* (Cambridge: Cambridge University Press).

LAUDAN, L. (1977) *Progress and Its Problems: Towards a Theory of Scientific Growth* (London: Routledge & Kegan Paul).

LEIJONHUFVUD, A. (1976) 'Schools, "Revolutions" and Research Programmes in Economic Theory', in S. J. Latsis (ed.), *Method and Appraisal in Economics* (Cambridge: Cambridge University Press).

LEONTIEF, W. (1983) Foreword to Eichner A. S. (ed.), *Why Economics is Not Yet a Science* (London: Macmillan).

LESTER, R. A. (1946) 'Shortcomings of Marginal Analysis for Wage Employment Problems', *American Economic Review*, vol. 36, March, pp. 62–82.

LIPSEY, R. G. (1963) *An Introduction to Positive Economics*, 1st edn (London: Weidenfeld & Nicolson).

LOASBY, B. J. (1984) 'On Scientific Method', *Journal of Post-Keynesian Economics*, vol. 6, no. 3, pp. 394–410.

McCLOSKEY, D. N. (1983) 'The Rhetoric of Economics', *Journal of Economic Literature*, vol. 21, June, pp. 481–517.

MACHLUP, F. (1946) 'Marginal Analysis and Empirical Research', *American Economic Review*, vol. 36, September, pp. 519–54.

McLACHLAN, H. V. and SWALES, J. K. (1982) 'Friedman's Methodology: A Comment on Boland', *Journal of Economic Studies*, vol. 9, no. 1, pp. 19–34.

McMULLIN, E. (1979) 'Discussion Review: Laudan's Progress and Its Problems', *Philosophy of the Social Sciences*, vol. 46, pp. 623–44.

MANDEL, E. (1976) Introduction to Marx (1976) *Capital* (Harmondsworth: Penguin).

MANDEL, E. (1983) 'Economics' in McLellan D. (ed.), *Marx: The First 100 Years* (London: Fontana).

MARCHI, N. DE (1976) 'Anomaly and the Development of Economics: the Case of the Leontief Paradox' in S. J. Latsis (ed.) *Method and Appraisal in Economics* (Cambridge: Cambridge University Press).

MARX, K. (1975) *Karl Marx: Texts on Method*, trans. and ed. by T. Carver (Oxford: Basil Blackwell).

MARX, K. (1976) *Capital: A Critique of Political Economy*, vol. 1, (Harmondsworth: Penguin).

MARX, K. (1981) *Capital: A Critique of Political Economy*, vol. 3, (Harmondsworth: Penguin).

MASTERMAN, M. (1970) 'The Nature of a Paradigm', from I. Lakatos and A. Musgrave (eds), *Criticism and the Growth of Knowledge* (Cambridge: Cambridge University Press).

MAXWELL, N. (1972) 'A Critique of Popper's View on Scientific Method', *Philosophy of Science*, vol. 39, pp. 131–52.

MAYER, T. (1980) 'Economics as Hard Science: Realistic Goal or Wishful Thinking?', *Economic Inquiry*, vol. 18, April, pp. 165–78.

MEDAWAR, P. B. (1969) *Induction and Intuition in Scientific Thought* (London: Methuen).

MEHTA, G. (1977) *The Structure of the Keynesian Revolution* (London: Martin Robertson).

MEHTA, G. (1979) 'The Keynesian Revolution', *International Journal of Social Economics*, vol. 6, no. 3, pp. 151–63.

MILLER, W. L. (1971) 'Richard Jones: A Case Study in Methodology', *History of Political Economy*, vol. 3, no. 1, pp. 198–207.

MILLS, F. C. (1924) 'On Measurement in Economics', in R. G. Tugwell (ed.), *The Trend in Economics* (New York: Alfred A. Knopf).

MISES, L. von (1962) *The Ultimate Foundation of Economic Science: An Essay on Method* (New York: Van Nostrand).

MISES, L. von (1966) *Human Action: A Treatise on Economics*, 3rd revised edn (Chicago, Ill.: Contemporary Books).

MISES, L. von (1976) *Epistemological Problems of Economics* (New York: New York University Press).

MISES, L. von (1978) *Ludwig von Mises, Notes and Recollections* (South Holland, Ill.: Libertarian Press).

MUSGRAVE, A. (1976) 'Method or Madness?' in R. S. Cohen, P. K. Feyerabend, and M. W. Wartofsky (eds), *Essays in Memory of Imre Lakatos* (Dordrecht: D. Reidal).

MUSGRAVE, A. (1979) 'Problems with Progress', *Synthese*, vol. 42, pp. 443–64.

MUSGRAVE, A. (1981) ' "Unreal Assumptions" in Economic Theory: the F-Twist Untwisted', *Kyklos*, vol. 34, pp. 377–87.

NAGEL, E. (1963) 'Assumptions in Economic Theory', *American Economic Review, Papers and Proceedings*, vol. 53, May, pp. 211–19.

NEILL, T. P. (1944) 'The Physiocrats concept of Economics', *Quarterly Journal of Economics*, vol. 63, November, pp. 532–53.

NEWTON-SMITH, W. H. (1981) *The Rationality of Science* (London: Routledge & Kegan Paul).

O'DRISCOLL, G. P. and RIZZO, M. J. (1985) *The Economics of Time and Ignorance* (Oxford: Basil Blackwell).

O'HEAR, A. (1980) *Karl Popper* (London: Routledge & Kegan Paul).

PESARAN, M. H. and SMITH, R. (1985) 'Keynes On Econometrics', in T. Lawson and M. H. Pesaran (eds), *Keynes' Economics: Methodological Issues* (London: Croom Helm).

PHEBY, J. (1985) 'Keynes on Econometrics', paper presented at History of Economics Society Conference (Fairfax, Va.: George Mason University).

PHEBY, J. (1986) 'Economic Methodology at the Crossroads', *British Review of Economic Issues*, vol. 18, Spring, pp. 99–105.

PILLING, G. (1980) *Marx's Capital: Philosophy and Political Economy* (London: Routledge & Kegan Paul).

POPPER, K. R. (1970) 'Normal Science and its Dangers' in I. Lakatos and A. Musgrave (eds), *Criticism and the Growth of Knowledge* (Cambridge: Cambridge University Press).

POPPER, K. R. (1972) *Conjectures and Refutations: The Growth of Scientific Knowledge*, 4th edn (London: Routledge & Kegan Paul).

POPPER, K. R. (1976a) *Unended Quest: An Intellectual Autobiography* (London: Fontana/Collins).

POPPER, K. R. (1976b) *The Poverty of Historicism* (London: Routledge & Kegan Paul).

POPPER, K. R. (1983) *Realism and the Aim of Science*, (London: Hutchinson).

PREST, A. R. (1983) 'Letter to a Young Economist', *Economic Affairs*, January, pp. 130–4.

PRIBRAM, K. (1983) *A History of Economic Reasoning* (Baltimore: Johns Hopkins University Press).

PUTNAM, H. (1981) 'The "Corroboration" of Theories', in I. Hacking (ed.), *Scientific Revolutions* (Oxford: Oxford University Press).

RASHID, S. (1979) 'Richard Jones and Baconian Historicism at Cambridge', *Journal of Economic Issues*, vol. 13, March, pp. 159–73.

REMENYI, D. V. (1979) 'Core demi-core interaction: toward a general theory of disciplinary and subdisciplinary growth', *History of Political Economy*, vol. 11, no. 1, pp. 30–63.

RICARDO, D. (1952) *The Works and Correspondence of David Ricardo*, P. Sraffa (ed.) *Vol. VI, Letters 1810–1815*, Royal Economic Society (Cambridge: Cambridge University Press).

RIZZO, M. J. (1982) 'Mises and Lakatos: A Reformulation of Austrian Methodology' in I. Kirzner (ed.), *Method, Process and Austrian Economics: Essays in Honour of Ludwig von Mises* (Lexington, Mass.: D. C. Heath).

ROBBINS, L. (1971) *Autobiography of an Economist* (London: Macmillan).

ROBBINS, L. (1981) 'Economics and Political Economy' *AEA Papers and Proceedings*, vol. 71, no. 2, pp. 1–10.

ROSDOLSKY, R. (1980) *The Making of Marx's Capital* (London: Pluto Press).

ROTHBARD, M. N. (1976) 'Praxeology: The Methodology of Austrian Economics' in E. G. Dolan (ed.), *The Foundations of Modern Austrian Economics* (Kansas City: Sheed and Ward).

RUTHERFORD, M. (1984) 'Rational Expectations and Keynesian Uncertainty: a Critique', *Journal of Post-Keynesian Economics*, vol. 6, no. 3, Spring, pp. 377–87.

SAYER, D. (1983) *Marx's Method: Ideology, Science and Critique in 'Capital'*, 2nd edn (Brighton: Harvester Press).

SCHUMPETER, J. A. (1954) *History of Economic Analysis* (New York: Oxford University Press).

SHACKLE, G. L. S. (1972) *Epistemics and Economics* (Cambridge: Cambridge University Press).

SHACKLE, G. L. S. (1974) *Keynesian Kaleidics* (Edinburgh: Edinburgh University Press).

SHAPERE, D. (1971) 'The Paradigm Concept', *Science*, vol. 172, pp. 706–9.

SHAW, G. K. (1984) *Rational Expectations: An Elementary Exposition* (Brighton: Wheatsheaf Books).

SHERMAN, H. (1981) 'Marx and Determinism', *Journal of Economic Issues*, vol. 14, March, pp. 61–71.

SPADARO, L. M. (1978) 'Toward a Program of Research and Development for Austrian Economics' in L. M. Spadaro (ed.), *New Directions in Austrian Economics* (Kansas City: Sheed Andrews and McMeel).

STANFIELD, R. (1974) 'Kuhnian Revolutions and the Keynesian Revolution', *Journal of Economic Issues*, vol. 8, March, pp. 97–109.

STIGLER, G. (1969) 'Does Economics Have a Useful Past?' *History of Political Economy*, vol. 1, pp. 217–30.

TARASCIO, V. J. and CALDWELL, B. J. (1979) 'Theory Choice in Economics: Philosophy and Practice', *Journal of Economic Issues*, vol. 13, December, pp. 983–1006.

THUROW, L. C. (1983) *Dangerous Currents: the State of Economics* (Oxford: Oxford University Press).

WARD, B. (1972) *What's Wrong with Economics?* (London: Macmillan).

WATKINS, J. W. N. (1968) 'Methodological Individualism and Social Tendencies' in Brodbeck M. (ed.), *Readings in the Philosophy of the Social Sciences*, (London: Collier-Macmillan).

WATKINS, J. W. N. (1970) 'Against "Normal Science"' in I. Lakatos and A. Musgrave (eds), *Criticism and the Growth of Knowledge* (Cambridge: Cambridge University Press).

WEDBERG, A. (1982) *A History of Philosophy, Vol. 2, The Modern Age of Romanticism* (Oxford: Oxford University Press).

WILES, P. (1983) 'Ideology, Methodology and Neoclassical Economics', from A. S. Eichner (ed.), *Why Economics is Not Yet a Science* (London: Macmillan).

WOLFE, A. B. (1924) 'Functional Economics' in R. G. Tugwell (ed.), *The Trend in Economics* (New York: Alfred A. Knopf).

WORRALL, J. (1976) 'Imre Lakatos (1922–1974) "Philosopher of Mathematics and Philosopher of Science"' in R. S. Cohen, P. K. Feyerabend and M. W. Wartofsky (eds), *Essays in Memory of Imre Lakatos*, Dordrecht: D. Reidel.

ZELENÝ, J. (1980) *The Logic of Marx* (Oxford: Basil Blackwell).

ZELLNER, A. (1979) 'Causality and Econometrics' in K. Brunner and A. H. Meltzer (eds), *Three Aspects of Policy and Policymaking: Knowledge, Data and Institutions*, supplement to vol. 10 of the Journal of Monetary Economics.

Name Index

Subject Index